SEA

*Niemen*

Bay of
Gdansk

Kaliningrad

Sztutowo

*Pregola*

Czerniachowsk

*Wilia*

Wilno
(Vilnius)

Lidzbark
Warminski

Gizycko

Olsztyn

Biskupiec

Elk

Augustow

*Niemen*

udziadz

n

*Biebrza*

*Narew*

Bialystok

Bielsk Podlaski

*Vistula*

*Narew*

*Bug*

Plock

Treblinka

Bialowieza

U.S.S.R.

Zelazowa Wola

WARSAW

*Bug*

utno

Lowicz

Piasecznno

Otwock

Janow Podlaski

Brzesc

Skolimow-Konstancin

Garwolin

*Prypec*

Lodz

Maciejowice

Ryki

*Pilica*

Deblin

Radom

Pulawy

Sobibor

Zwolen

Kazimierz

*Warta*

Lublin

Majdanek

*Bug*

ochowa

Kielce

Chelm

Checiny

Jedrzejow

*Vistula*

Zamosc

*San*

om

Belzec

siemianowice

Sosnowiec

Mysl. Cracow

Rzeszow

Jaroslaw

owice

Nowa Huta

uschwitz

Wieliczka

Tarnow

Oświęcim)

Przemysl

Lwow
(Lvov)

*Dniestr*

Zakopane

MOUNTAINS

0        50        100 Miles

HOSLOVAKIA

0     50     100     150 Km.

# POLAND: EAGLE IN THE EAST

*Also by William Woods*

The Edge of Darkness

The Street of Seven Monks

The Mask

Riot at Gravesend

Manuela

A Yugoslav Adventure

A Mermaid in Nikoli

# Poland: EAGLE IN THE EAST

*A Survey of Modern Times by*

WILLIAM WOODS

 HILL AND WANG · NEW YORK

To  KIT

who lived through it all with me,
sometimes under great difficulties,
but always with courage, loyalty, and love.

# Preface

I must begin, as they say in Parliament, by confessing an interest. In the winter of 1966–67 I was approached by a representative of the Polish government temporarily in London, and asked if I would be willing to go to Warsaw and gather material for a book to be written about contemporary Poland. They felt that too little was known in the West about their country.

I was promised every possible cooperation, an opportunity to go where I pleased, meet whom I pleased, and of course, in the end, to write what I pleased. There was only one proviso, that I, in my turn, would undertake so far as I was able to look at things in the perspective of Polish history and with an awareness of Poland's particular economic and political problems. They would promise not to attempt to censor what I wrote in any way. I would promise simply to be as fair and objective as I was able.

PREFACE

I have spent a frustrated, fascinating, maddening, and delightful year and a half at this book. The Poles kept their promise. I traveled perhaps ten thousand miles inside the country and talked to—it may be—over a thousand people, Catholics and atheists, churchmen, peasant farmers, workers in factories, artists, actors, industrial managers, experts of one sort or another, economic planners, fishermen, shipyard workers, students, politicans, and even prisoners. I met many who supported the regime and many who loathed it.

Very early I learned to mistrust journalistic generalizations, for I read articles in our Western press which (whatever their politics) I recognized from my own experience to be far too superficial to have got anywhere near the truth. And it took little time at all to learn just how huge a task I had set myself. For whoever would write a book about modern Poland ought to have a sound understanding of all European history (even to the letters of Pope Clement V), and particularly of all the peculiar and indeed unique problems that Poland herself has had to face. He ought to know intimately the history of Hitler's war and of the twenty-three years that have passed since it ended, to understand current political and economic theory, the problems of agriculture and industrialization, not only in Poland, but elsewhere, of chemistry, mineralogy, transport and the migrations of peoples, above all, of human psychology, the tormented self-analysis of those who have suffered, the anger and impatience of those who have not.

When he has learned to understand these things, then
he ought to look, to read, to listen, to evaluate, and above
all learn to beware as he would of the devil of over-
simplification. To write about Poland is to walk on eggs,
and this is a book I shall wish for the rest of my life I
could rewrite, modify, clarify, and strengthen. No one
ever knows half what he should about a subject, so I do
not pretend, heaven knows, invariably to have been right
about this one. But I have tried invariably to be fair and
to put things into perspective.

After a few weeks of traveling around Poland, the
parts or divisions of the book fell very naturally into
place. It had to begin with the war. Politics, economics,
agriculture, the arts, the very psyche of the people were
conditioned almost beyond anything we can imagine by
Hitler's invasion, slaughter, and humiliation of the nation. It is probably true to say that the strongest cohesive
force in Poland today, second, of course, to a sense of
nationality, is a loathing of the Germans. That is why I
have devoted more space to the war than might seem
desirable to an outside observer.

Of course, with the reestablishment of peace in 1945,
reconstruction was of paramount importance, and then,
it seemed to me, the simplest course for the writer was to
treat various aspects of Polish life and contemporary history more or less in the order of their importance to the
Poles. Thus industrialization, agriculture, the Church, the
arts—each always in relationship to the ubiquitous Party
—fell into place one by one.

In February and March 1968, I went back again, by great good luck in time for the student demonstrations and the enormous political ferment these aroused. And one difficulty was that by that time I could just as well understand the sense of the Central Committee as I could that of the students who demonstrated against it. The one were certainly not faceless beasts. Nor were the others dupes of the Zionists or anyone else.

Now I have had to stop my history in midstream—except that events never come to a conclusion anyway. We are always in midstream, and it would be wrong, even if I could, to present here certain pages with the implication that they defined a people, a nation, and offered them up, neatly analyzed and wrapped in a cloth binding. No, sociology, economics, politics, thinking, the very ethos of any people will always evolve. The good and the wicked in contemporary Poland will tomorrow be different. So mine does not pretend by any means to be the final word.

With some very few exceptions, I was met wherever I went with an enormous courtesy and kindness. People tumbled over each other to talk about Poland, for Poles love their country with what to us seems unusual fervor. Occasionally, of course, there were those like the Leninist club of students near Cracow who attacked differing opinions with all the loud, irrational stubbornness of doctrinaire Chinese, or the Interpress representative, Mr. Prejss of Gdansk, who had been asked to be my guide in the city, but who turned out to be simply and gratuitously rude.

But everywhere else, from Lublin to Szczecin and Mazuria to Wroclaw, and particularly in Kazimierz and Warsaw I was met with the gentleness and open-handed helpfulness and hospitality which are my pleasantest memories of this sad, exhilarating, complex, and beautiful country. To many anonymous souls I offer here my thanks, but I want to single out for her most especial assistance Mrs. Anna Broniarek, a friend to my wife and me, a woman intense, knowledgeable, violently patriotic, stubborn, thorough, and helpful beyond the call of duty. How many hours we quarreled about various aspects of her country I do not know, but (dear Anna) we never had an argument that failed to teach me something.

In a word, the Poles did as they promised. I very much hope they will think I have done the same.

WILLIAM WOODS

*The Old Vicarage,*
*Glasbury-on-Wye,*
*Radnorshire*
*May 11, 1968*

# Contents

PHOTOGRAPHS FOLLOW PAGE 144.

POLAND: EAGLE IN THE EAST

# 1. Poland 1939 — Defeat

ALL CITIES, certainly all of the great cities, have sad and ugly places in them—scrag ends of streets, perhaps—and these are generally in the older parts of town, and nothing has changed in such districts since anyone can remember.

But the sadness of Warsaw, which is one of those splendid cities like hawks perched on the borders of two cultures, one of the chain running across Eastern Europe like Vienna, Budapest, Belgrade, bulwarks against Byzantium, the sadness of Warsaw lies in the fact that nothing old is left of it. The Germans blew it up street by street and so gutted it that by Christmas 1944 there was not a soul left alive there, nothing but rats and ruins.

As a result, no one has lived in Warsaw more than a generation. Most of the houses have gone up in the memory of any schoolboy, and in spite of the white Polish eagle, in spite of Tannenberg, Chopin, and Copernicus, fifty years ago Warsaw had not even an independent state to wrap around itself. Yet even then, because of its charm, its flair, its sense of style, its romanticism, and perpetual nostalgia, they called it the Paris of the East.

Over a thousand years ago Mieszko I, whose kingdom had frontiers remarkably similar to those of modern Poland, accepted Christianity, not so much out of conviction as out of a very practical fear that unless he did so Christ would come carried in on the sword arms of his German neighbors. Poles already had had experience of the Tartars. In other words, even then the pattern had been established of a Poland sandwiched between bigger and more powerful enemies, a Poland that bowed but never broke.

By the thirteenth century it was Muscovy and those same Tartars to the east, a Germany full of colonizing zeal to the west, to the north the savage Teutonic Knights and the unfriendly sea. Several hundred years later the Teutonic Knights had been beaten, but Sweden took their place, seized the Oder estuary, and sold it to the Prussians. Later still, the Hapsburg empire to the south, like some vast, divisible amoeba, began spreading up past the Vistula into what is now Russian territory. And always in the center, Poles, the people of the plain (the word *pole* means field), the farmers and breeders of horses, with a weak monarchy that made for decentralization, a multitudinous minor gentry that made the towns impotent and prevented even their growth, the soil sandy and lean, the whole still a peasant economy chopped into tiny parcels (and thus ripe for conquest by its stronger neighbors) when all the rest of Europe was being industrialized.

But I was talking about the sadness of Warsaw now, and to explain it, to see modern Poland, one has to start by going back at least a generation. It is only in the past generation (and this quite apart from one's own political ideology) that Poland has for the first time in a thousand years begun to fulfill the promise of its generous, diverse, chaotic, brilliantly talented, and imaginative people, a people quite unlike any other in the world, for their talk is almost invariably witty and their songs are almost invariably sad.

So let us start a generation ago, with Hitler's war. Nations have been defeated before, but never in modern history has a nation suffered not only defeat, but also such slaughter of its best and such sustained and terrible humiliation.

One must go back to the war, too, because what Germany did then produced not only a physical, but also a psychic aftermath. Even in forty or fifty years, when the fear and hatred have died away, new generations will still look at Germans with a certain uneasiness. Therefore no survey of modern Poland would even be coherent unless the part Germany played in the nation's destruction and the dread of Germany during Poland's subsequent rebirth were both made abundantly plain.

For the people of Warsaw, war began in earnest on

the sixth of September 1939, five days after Hitler had attacked, when the government announced that the enemy had broken the Polish lines. All able-bodied men were to flee to the east, for the Russians had not yet moved forward to the first of what eventually proved to be three new frontiers that Ribbentrop and Molotov had worked out between them. The Polish leaders themselves made off to Lublin with the national gold reserve —nine days later they had reached the Rumanian border —and in Warsaw left only the mayor, a calm and splendid man called Starzynski, in authority.

Up in the Corridor, General von Kluge's Fourth Army pushed east from Pomerania and General von Küchler's Third Army west from East Prussia, and there, according to William Shirer,[1] occurred one of the most bizarre episodes of the short campaign. Today Polish authorities deny the story, as though they were ashamed. But Shirer says that General Guderian, racing eastward with his tanks, suddenly found himself being counterattacked by the Polish Pomorska Brigade of cavalry. Cavalrymen with lances couched charging down upon tanks.

Overhead, fighter planes roaring, on the ground a whole division of armor, on the roads, self-propelled guns—and against these a magnificent but suicidal charge of Polish cavalry.

Up on the coast outside Gdansk, another almost in-

[1] William L. Shirer, *The Rise and Fall of the Third Reich*, Simon and Schuster, New York, 1960.

[ 4 ]

credible feat of heroism. The garrison at Westerplatte guarding Gdansk harbor, a hundred and eighty-six men with a few mortars and an old French cannon, were still holding out against Stuka divebombers and the cruiser *Schleswig Holstein*. One has to have seen that shallow, sandy promontory to realize just how brave and hopeless an encounter it must have been.

Elsewhere there was only chaos and the last great battle at Kutno to be fought. Poland was in fact already beaten—more rapidly than even the Germans had expected—and at the end of September (shells were already falling in Warsaw) Mayor Starzynski went to the radio and spoke a quiet, passionate appeal for patience and unity. He told his listeners that they now had no choice except to wait and see it through to better days. It was one of the greatest understatements ever made.

For Hitler had said, "I keep my Death's Head Battalions ready without mercy or pity to kill men, women and children of Polish origin. That is the only way we shall get the living space we need." This on the twenty-second of August, ten days before the war had even started.

A little over a month later, on the twenty-seventh of September, the Germans entered Warsaw and began to act on their leader's pronouncement. Mayor Starzynski was arrested and shortly afterward shot. Up north in Gdansk where the post office workers had held out as long as their ammunition lasted, they too, when they surrendered, were marched out, and by express order of the German commandant, General Friedrich Eberhardt, stood up against a wall and murdered. The excuse was that they were not in regular army uniforms. In many towns, in Katowice, in Kornik, in Bydgoszcz, and Czestochowa, leading citizens, some because they had taken part in the Silesian rebellion of 1921, some whose only offense was to possess a university degree, were dragged out of their houses and arbitrarily hanged or stood up before firing squads. All in all, some thousands of men and women—lawyers, petty officials, doctors, clergymen, and simple housewives—were either marched to a wall or strung up, dangling in long rows in the public market place. It had been no idle threat on Hitler's part. The slaughter and humiliation had started and Germany had begun as she intended to go on.

Her plan, never secret, but openly announced, was to smother any possible resistance before it could even be organized, but first of all to keep her enemies divided. Thus Ruthenian was to be set against Czech, Ukrainian against Pole, townsman against countryman, Catholic against Jew. To this end, no Polish child was to be taught anything beyond the most elementary reading and arithmetic. In the rump Polish state that remained (the Government General under the command of Hans Frank), schooling was permitted up to the fourth form, but not beyond. In the rest of Poland there were no schools at all.

Priests, soldiers, teachers, lawyers, leaders of any sort were to be annihilated. People of education particularly were to be put down, and in fact, only 60 per cent of Poles who had university degrees survived the war. The entire plan was never fulfilled, but Hitler's intention was that in time approximately half the Polish nation, which numbered just under thirty-five million, was to be murdered and the remainder, reduced to the status of mutes and slaves, was to serve as mobile labor for the Third Reich.

Yet during the early days of the occupation a stranger would have thought life in Warsaw astonishingly normal, for quantitative murder takes time to organize. The city lies on both sides of the wide and shallow Vistula, the left bank, as in London or Paris, being the more lively. There the broad Lazienki Gardens where nowadays Chopin is played on summer Sundays, the enchanting little Lazienki Palace, there the unusually wide shopping streets—Jerozolimskie running westward from the Poniatowski Bridge and, crossing it north and south, the elegant Nowy Swiat, or New World Street, as well as Krakowskie Przedmiescie and Krucza and Marszalkowska with their big stores and clanging trams. Up along the riverbank, the great Warsaw Castle overlooking the Stare Miasto, or Old Town, with pink, green, and yellow pastel houses on the squares, with coachmen waiting for late customers at the Krokodyl, with wine shops old as Warsaw itself and the great brick Cathedral of St. John where eventually Hitler was to stable his horses.

It was and is a green city of over a million people, a noisy, talkative, dusty city proud of its chic. Nursemaids wheeled children out into the parks or under the old trees in Emilia Plater. And even after the German army had arrived, the noisy, ubiquitous tramcars clanged down Marszalkowska. Honeysuckle grew in the Lazienki Gardens and the fountain changed color at the top of the long steps there with the new moon dying monthly behind it.

The girls were strikingly handsome, long-legged and blonde as Polish girls have always been. Here and there, to be sure, a sign reading: *Jews not admitted*. Radios had been confiscated, too. But banks opened every morning. Trains and busses ran as usual. Postmen went their rounds, and in the restaurants there was music and plenty to eat. Cinemas were open too, but the underground had asked people not to attend them (and watch the German newsreels), so they remained empty.

What no stranger could have sensed was a new feeling in the city of interdependence and solidarity. People quite unknown to each other offered one another food or (if a man was caught out after curfew) a night's lodging. Early on the RAF began dropping forged Polish zlotys for the use of the Home Army, and these were never stolen but generally found their way to their destination.

In the beginning the Germans retaliated against these forgeries by calling in all notes to have them stamped with a guarantee of genuineness. The Poles answered by forging the stamps. At one time (according to an official in the present Ministry of Finance) there were actually seventeen varieties of forgery in circulation, four of these so well made that the Germans never detected them for the duration of the war.

In the end the RAF put an end to the game by dropping dollars instead, for actually the Polish zloty notes made in England had been a bit dangerous to handle. The paper had been too good. As for the dollars, they were quoted like shares in the market, falling when the news was bad, rising when it improved. But in a time of chaotically rising prices they were at least a reasonably stable currency.

For inflation did start very early in the war. The zloty had been four to the dollar, sixteen to the pound sterling, and in 1939—to take a few prices at random—ham had cost about five zlotys a kilogram, sugar one zloty, butter about five again, bacon approximately three, lunch in a good restaurant two zlotys, and a suit of clothes sixty zlotys. In eighteen months, by the spring of 1941, these prices had risen tenfold, except for the suit, which could not be bought for love or money.

So workmen, the average of whose wages in that same year and a half had only risen from two hundred to five hundred zlotys a month, began stealing from factories to supplement their incomes, and since factories were largely working for the German war effort, these thefts were excused to oneself as a form of sabotage as well.

Once every week or so housewives would go off into the country to buy food from peasants and smuggle it back into town for use or resale. When the Home Army had become sufficiently well organized, it stole from German supply trains, generally uncoupling a wagon at night and rolling it into a siding, so periodically Warsaw was flooded with the most bizarre and unexpected commodities. One month it would be fur coats diverted from the Russian front, or woolen socks and pullovers knitted by good German *Hausfrauen*. Once it was a shipment of turtles intended to be turned into soup for the Wehrmacht, and since no one could bear to kill them (and thus act like a German), almost every household acquired its own pet.

In the winter of 1940–41 there began to be a serious shortage of electricity. One side of a street would get current for half the month, the other side for the second half. Coal was hard to come by too, and the average winter temperature in Poland is well below freezing. So people made do with candles and carbide lamps, in which there was of course a flourishing black market.

A market sometimes almost for the sake of a market. If you needed shoes you might buy glass because you had heard of a man who was demolishing a shed to make a greenhouse (there was profit in vegetables) and had timber to dispose of, which in turn you could sell to a carpenter whose brother (the grapevine told you) had somewhere managed to "find" several hundred pairs of Rumanian shoes intended for export to Germany. There was in fact one famous crate of candles in the Powisle district which changed hands eight or ten times—until the ultimate buyer discovered to his horror that they had no wicks.

"Don't worry about such a minor point," he was told. "They weren't meant to be used anyway. Only to be bartered."

Almost overnight the habits, the way of life of the average Warsovian had undergone a change. Chalk drawings of tortoises appeared on the walls to serve as reminders that it was unpatriotic to work too hard. Work was scarce anyway, except that which helped the Germans, so everyone "fiddled" instead, bought or sold currency, gold, jewelry, German *Kennkarten*, or identification cards, and this buying and selling became a veritable way of life.

Journalists, actors, artists turned themselves into waiters in the ubiquitous cafes. Society ladies became cooks and opened lunchtime restaurants. It was the only thing they knew how to do, and of course the curfew had made any sort of night life impossible. The whole city developed a passion for playing bridge; several famous cafes set aside rooms for the players. And in every such public place, music, for most musicians were otherwise unemployed. So on the surface at least, life looked even more gay and frivolous than before the war.

There was a huge trade in rare books, antiques, *objets d'art* (anything English fetched a particularly high price), and this, while it made the shops look positively luxurious, was of course a symptom of the general malaise, the same that had made cooks out of countesses.

People were simply selling whatever they could lay hands on to buy food.

A curious contradiction that Warsaw occupied should seem a good deal more glittering than Warsaw free. Everything, it seemed, was prohibited—and most things had become possible if one knew how to set about it. The Germans put up signs forbidding the sale of white bread under pain of death. And under the notices old women sat—and sold white bread.

But on the evening after Christmas 1939 there came a far more sinister development. Of course people had heard tales of atrocities in the provinces, but the facts had never really been brought home to them. Then, on the night of the twenty-sixth of December, a German soldier was killed in a brawl out in the suburb of Wawer. With frightening speed a hundred and seven Poles were arrested quite at random, dragged off one particular commuter train, or out of their beds, and shot in reprisal.

In Wawer that night women milled around in the dark, regardless of curfew, looking for their husbands or their sons. And for the first time people began to realize that no relationship was possible with their conquerors except that of animal and hunter, and that if the war lasted long enough one was going to have to be both clever and lucky to survive. They did not yet know that the war was going to last over five and a half years, and that before it ended half the population of Warsaw was going to die.

Thereafter, on frosty mornings when people trudged to work past the legless soldiers begging in the wide and lovely Krakowskie Przedmiescie, or the street musicians in Krucza, or the beggar children singing at windy corners everywhere, thereafter they had only one word for each other, one hope.

Wait until spring, they said. When spring comes the French and British will attack. Tomorrow will be better, for it most assuredly cannot be worse.

# 2. Plunder — The Jews

Iᴛ ᴡᴀs a shock to Professor Stanislaw Lorentz of the National Museum when he first had it brought home to him that it was not only louts and thugs who had taken to pillage and murder. Behind their façades of respectability, German intellectuals were actually hoodlums too.

Early in November 1939, Professor Dagobert Frey of Vienna and Breslau turned up in his office. Frey was well known to him, was a fellow art historian, and had as such been given complete freedom before the war to study the Polish collections. He turned out to have made thorough notes and he knew exactly what he wanted. He had come now not to pay a social call, simply to hand over a list of the pictures that were to be removed.[1]

---

[1] "I can still see Professor Frey, whom I had known well before the war, admiring the beauty of a neo-classic fireplace . . . and in my

Hans Frank, the Governor General, picked up a number of priceless objects for his own use, notably Leonardo's "Lady with a Weasel," in Cracow. But one expected that of the SS. One did not expect it of writers in learned journals, of men like Dr. Posse, director of the famous Dresden gallery; but he turned out to be a thief like many other Germans. There were scores of them, all with official licenses to steal. One of the last was a certain infamous Sturmbannführer, who combined his vulgarity with a certain moral righteousness. With his own hands he destroyed about a thousand modern works of art he considered degenerate. He hacked up paintings, sculptures, even the floors. According to Professor Lorentz (though I have not been able to confirm the fact) this Sturmbannführer survived the war and is now living in West Germany.

Nor was this all. Warsaw Castle, the former royal residence and a veritable museum of the baroque and the neoclassic, was systematically plundered, the ceilings cut out with saws, the beams and furnishings simply hurled out of the windows. Members of the staff of the National Museum tried to save whatever they could, ceilings, sculptures, woodcarvings, bits of stucco decora-

---

presence giving the order to have it torn away from the wall. Professor Frey had been my guest before the war. In January, 1939, I had been his. In July of that year we had travelled through England together by car to the international congress of art historians. Now, not even three months later, quite without shame and in the presence of his Polish colleagues, he could demolish our Polish national monument." Stanislaw Lorentz, *The Destruction of Warsaw Castle*, Warsaw, 1947.

tion. It was in vain. The Germans forbade anything to be taken out of the building except by German workmen.

At one time, on the other hand, any German stationed in Warsaw, military or civilian, was allowed to take away whatever souvenirs he could carry. So tapestries, busts, paintings, all went west to testify to the earnestness and perceptiveness of German *Kultur*. But when two Poles tried to take photographs of the building to help in its eventual reconstruction, they were arrested and imprisoned by the Gestapo.

When the castle had been thoroughly gutted, some ten thousand holes were drilled in the walls and filled with explosives. Five years afterward, in December 1944, when Warsaw had become a deserted city and the castle could no longer serve any conceivable purpose, it was blown up.

Another of the German acts of destruction was even more self-obsessed. Away to the west near Poznan, architects had some ten or twelve years before discovered the remains of several prehistoric Slavic settlements. When the Germans moved in, their experts examined these sites and decided they had really been Germanic in origin. Slavs supposedly had never had the training and craftsmanship to build structures as complex as these were seen to have been. When, however, further investigation showed the buildings to have been Slavic after all, they were simply destroyed. The ground was leveled. If they were Slavic in origin they could be of no possible interest to future archaeologists.

All during the war Lorentz and a few courageous helpers worked to save what they could from the almost universal ruin. First of all, catalogues were kept of the works looted and, when possible, notes were made of the destinations in Germany to which they had been sent. Second, what could be hidden was hidden, sometimes in cellars in Warsaw, sometimes in provincial towns. And third, when it became plain that the Germans were systematically destroying old buildings, they took endless photographs to be used in their eventual reconstruction.

Then in 1940 when the first concentration camps had been erected on Polish soil (there had of course been camps in Germany for six or seven years before that) the Germans were able to start carrying out their plans for extermination on a wider scale. At the most unexpected times, without apparent rhyme or reason, there would come the order for a *lapanka*, a roundup. Twenty or thirty SS men would swarm into a cafe, demanding papers. If your *Ausweis* showed that you worked for the Germans or—strangely enough—in the Lazienki Gardens, you were allowed to slip through the net. If not, you were marched out into the street and in many cases never heard of again. Or a tram would be stopped, all the passengers ordered off and herded perhaps to the nearest wall where they might be lined up and shot. Or in the middle of the night the occupants of some huge

[ 17 ]

block of flats, men, women, and children, would be ordered down into the courtyards. An announcement would be read, according to which the building was needed for Germans, and by morning the Poles would find themselves in cattle trucks on the way to Auschwitz.[2]

The defeat of Norway in April 1940, had come as a shock, though Warsaw rumor had it that the British had tricked Hitler into overextending his lines of communication. But then had come the rapid German victories over Holland and Belgium and the terrible thought that it might be a long war after all. When on June fourteenth General von Küchler's Eighteenth Army entered Paris, and the BBC, the only voice everyone relied on, admitted the fact, Poles in Warsaw wept in the streets.

And yet, beaten though Poland was, her fight went on. Much has been made of the fact that she was the only conquered country that had no Quisling, no collaborator. But this is not entirely true. David Irving[3] says that a Warsaw "philosopher," one Tarlo-Mazinski, and a certain Wincenty Jastrzebski, who had once been Polish Vice-Minister of Finance for a period of four days (and whose name he misspells) approached the German Embassy in Paris, offering to form a national committee to collaborate with them, but that the Germans turned

---

[2] I use the name Auschwitz because as Auschwitz it is known all over the world. The proper name of the place is of course the Polish Oświęcim.

[3] David Irving, *Accident, the Death of General Sikorski*. William Kimber, London, 1967.

them down. The present Polish government knows nothing about any such approach, and indeed, Mr. Jastrzebski is living peaceably in Warsaw today.

But there *were* collaborators, although their efforts never really got off the ground. One was Leo Kozlowski who had been Prime Minister briefly in 1934. From the army of General Anders he went over to the Germans and was sent by them to Berlin, but before he could do any damage he was killed in an Allied air raid.

Then there was Wladislaw Studnicki, who had always been pro-German and who, aged about seventy in 1940, went to Berlin and sent Hitler a series of memoranda, offering to help. They were brushed aside as of no value.

Last of all, in 1944, there was a third attempt reminiscent of the never-never land in Hitler's bunker. Three men were involved this time. They were Ferdinand Goetel, a writer, president of the Polish Pen Club, and not to be confused with his brother who teaches at Warsaw University today. The second was Emil Skiwski, whose chief claim to fame was that he had written a monograph on G. K. Chesterton. The third was Feliks Burdecki, member of the right-wing National Democrats, an anti-Semitic writer on interplanetary travel. These three had a plan to organize Polish troops (indeed, the Polish nation) to fight on the German side against the advancing Russians. The Germans even sent them to Katyn to view the mass graves there. But again, nothing came of the plan.

The massacre in Katyn Forest does seem to have been

one of the few crimes against Poland of which the Germans were innocent. In March 1943, they uncovered the graves of some 9000 Polish officers who (many of them) had hands tied behind their backs, and all of whom had been shot in the back of the head. On these bodies they found diaries and letters, none dated later than April 1940—over a year before the German invasion of Russia.

The Russians of course denied that they had had anything to do with the murders. To the present Polish government it is a matter of acute embarrassment that the matter should be brought up again. Their spokesmen plead that at best the case is unproved. But one would hate to be brought to trial with such a mass of circumstantial evidence standing against one.

Today the vast majority of Poles are perfectly certain that the Russians were guilty of this crime, and in 1943 their knowledge of it only accentuated their loneliness. Except for an almost entirely ineffectual England, Poland had no friends.

People woke in the morning with the quite conscious thought that there was nowhere on earth to hide. One was surrounded by enemies and might not be alive by nightfall. The safety we take for granted, the protection of the police, for example, the money, the work, the influential acquaintances, the very reasonableness of normal existence and intercourse no longer held true. If a man was shot down in the street (and this happened often and unexpectedly) his very friends walked by and pretended not to notice. Yet (one saw it over and over again) wherever Poles were killed, on whatever pavement, within half an hour (and one never found out by whom) there were roses laid in the blood.

Poles fought in the RAF, and in such large numbers that during the Battle of Britain one enemy plane in seven was shot down by a Polish pilot. In Russia, General Anders held together a Polish army of 90,000 men, raised from among refugees after the Polish-Soviet treaty of 1941, and brought it out, first through Iran to Iraq, then to Egypt to fight on the side of the West. Poles were to fight at Tobruk, at Cassino, at Arnhem. Poles fought in the French underground. Even at home there were Polish troops, men who had simply not surrendered in 1939, men who had gone into hiding, workmen and peasants, men like Sgt. Iwanczyk (he called himself Stary Jakub) who led regular companies in the woods near Kielce. Very early they called themselves Armia Krajowa, or Home Army (to distinguish themselves from the Poles fighting abroad) and owed allegiance to the government in exile under General Sikorski in London.

At first their leadership, in the best Polish bureaucratic tradition, thought every village ought to have its own platoon. They kept files and records and became so overorganized that after a while even the peasant children knew who was a partisan and who was not. Today Stary Jakub cannot understand how they were not all slaughtered in the first few weeks. But the entire nation was behind them—and they were lucky.

Once in a very long while an RAF plane would come in to some dark field and land an engineer trained in demolition, or a Pole with radio transmitters and new ciphers fresh from London. Over in Lublin province there were other boys, other discharged soldiers who more and more often seemed to spring out of the very ground, who roamed the roads at night to cut telephone wires or perhaps to club down a German and make off with his rifle and uniform.

After the Nazi assault on Russia in June 1941, small units began forming behind the lines under Communist leadership too. They called themselves Gwardia Ludowa (or People's Guard), as distinct from the Home Army. By 1944 they had grown sufficiently in numbers to be known, not as Gwardia, but Armia Ludowa. Still others, purporting to be anti-German, but actually anti-Semitic and anti-Russian too, and known as NSZ (or National Armed Forces), roamed wood and hamlet and helped make of them a kind of lawless no-man's land. Last of all there was the Falanga, under the leadership of Boleslaw Piasecki. These were actively Fascist, and although Mr. Piasecki seems to have been locked up for a time by the Gestapo, his record is dubious in the extreme. He is a man of great importance in Poland today, so we shall look at him more closely when we come to the contemporary scene.

At any rate, these groups, chiefly the AK commanded

from London and the AL commanded from Moscow, formed what was at first vaguely anarchic resistance. Later they were to become organized, acquire weapons, fight regular two- and three-day engagements with German troops. In the early days there was still too little hope, too little prospect of any help from allies themselves hard pressed for resistance to be at all effective. Political parties there might be, and differences in opinion that ranged from the Marxian to the most arrant clerical reactionary. But in one thing the nation was almost entirely united (the Piaseckis of this world to the contrary), and that was in the desire—somehow, with guns, with words, with songs, however one could—to fight. Fantastic though it may seem, there is today no record of any leader (with the exception of the handful of nonentities mentioned above), any part of the population of whatever party, that considered even a partial collaboration.

As the months went by in Warsaw, food became a little scarcer, restrictions a little more onerous. In 1941 an edict was handed down according to which one had to have a travel permit for any journey of more than fifty kilometers, and the Germans began to search trains coming in from the suburbs. People caught carrying food were arrested and sent off to one of the camps.

Everyone who was able to do so acquired false papers, false *Kennkarten*, false ration cards. These entitled the bearer to a loaf every two days, half a pound of butter every two weeks (but you never found any) and the bread, when you did manage to lay hands on it, turned out to be inedible. Or you got what the Poles called *dźwienkowiec*, or sonorous bread, because whoever ate it could not for hours afterward stop farting.

Then in the summer of 1941, a fresh turn of the screw. Huge placards began appearing in the streets, and they read: JEWS MEAN LICE. Or there would be the drawing of a Jew, and across his face the word: TYPHUS. At the same time Jews were ordered to leave their flats or houses and find fresh accommodation in the Muranow district north of the city center.

How they were congregated there and eventually walled in is too well known to need repetition here. How Jews were brought in as to a collecting point from other towns, how month after month the old, the weak, the useless, the mothers with children were sent out in the transports, mostly to Treblinka, this too is known. Sometimes they lived in their ghetto twelve and fifteen to a room (the average was actually thirteen). Sometimes they starved and died in the streets. Children went out through the sewers or over the wall by night, scavenging. Sometimes these children escaped. Sometimes they were found and murdered.

It is not part of my purpose in this account to tell that story all over again. It has been well told elsewhere and will not be forgotten. But a few points ought nevertheless to be made.

The German record is of course so savage as to put that whole generation beyond the bounds even of animal behavior. As their apologists would have it, the barbarity was practiced by a few SS troops, or by the Latvians, the Ukrainians, the dead, by anyone except themselves.

It was in fact practiced by the ordinary Wehrmacht soldier too, by civil servants and the gendarmerie, by officials of the German government, by judges, by lawyers, by people who even today are still in positions of authority in the Federal Republic. I never heard of one German in Poland who protested at the time and, having traveled Poland from end to end, I have still not heard one story of a German who at that time ever did a Jew a kindness.

For centuries, generations of Polish kings had practiced religious tolerance, so Jews had migrated there from all over Europe and the Middle East. By 1939 they numbered roughly three and a half million (one tenth of the nation) and they had only just begun the long process of assimilation. As early as the fourteenth century, Casimir the Great had built a castle on a bluff overlooking the Vistula for Esterka, his Jewish mistress. A town called Kazimierz had grown up around it, an enchanting place almost a hundred miles upstream from Warsaw. By the time of the German invasion the vast majority of people living in Kazimierz were Jews. And interestingly enough, they were not merchants or middlemen, but peasant farmers who spoke neither Polish nor Yiddish, but an old-fashioned patois of their own. Never having heard this, I cannot describe it. They were lenders of money without interest. They were patrons of Polish artists, many of whom remember them with affection and gratitude even today. They seem to have been an intelligent and highly cultivated people. They were eventually murdered to a man.

But Lodz, Radom, Lublin, Bialystok, Tarnow, Cracow, Warsaw itself had enormous Jewish communities, and these were a different story, for in the main they kept to themselves. They were the old-fashioned Hassidic Jews who wore the caftan and often spoke little or no Polish. And in the fact that they were linguistically and even in their dress distinguishable from their neighbors lay the difficulty when later some of those neighbors tried to help them.

At the end of World War I the indigenous Jews were joined by others called Litvaks who had fled from Russian Poland. These either retained their old loyalty to the Tsar (perhaps because devout Jews were more often than not political conservatives), and so made enemies not only among the Galician and German Jews, but among the Poles as well, who after a hundred and fifty years of partition were trying desperately to shape a nation. Either this, or occasionally they were Communists, and to the middle and upper classes ruling Poland after the first war, Communists were anathema. But whether right or left wing, they were "un-Polish," and that was enough.

At the same time, irony of ironies, the Jews from German Poland aroused antagonism by their loyalty to Germany. The Jew, in short, too often seemed a friend to the partition which no Pole could bear, and this fact contributed not a little to the anti-Semitism which grew in Poland during the first four decades of the century.

Let me not be misunderstood. The separateness was always there. Among a nineteenth-century peasantry that belonged in the Middle Ages, fear and distrust of the Jew were always there. To the largely illiterate Polish serf (and we must remember that there was actually serfdom in Russian Poland as there was slavery in America until a little over a hundred years ago), to the serf the Jew was an enemy of his church, but in general, peasant and Jew shared an attitude of laissez faire. There were never pogroms in Poland as there were in Russia and Rumania. But in 1918 the Jew seemed to have become a friend to Poland's enemies, and that, for the normally illiterate Polish peasant, put him finally beyond the pale.

So during this latest war, the Polish record left much to be desired. There were, for example, Poles who betrayed and blackmailed Jews. When possible, let it be said at once, these informers were executed by the Home Army. There were Poles, on the other hand, who went into the ghettos, not only in Warsaw, but also in Cracow and Bialystok, and fought side by side with their fellow countrymen. Again, let it be said, these were mainly Communists. There were Poles who took Jewish children into their houses, and this was a crime which, when discovered, was punishable by death.

There were some who did even more. There were

Christian nurses and maidservants who actually accompanied their Jewish households into the ghettos and subsequently perished in the death camps.[4] There was a family called Marczak who hid thirty-four fugitives in a dugout under their vegetable garden in Grojecka Street in Warsaw. More than fifty Jews passed through the Warsaw house of Janina Szandorowska. Seventeen Jews were given asylum in the house of a certain Jozef Kaleta-Pirowska. Lucja and Stefan Slonimski hid ten Jews for more than two years.

In other words, there were hundreds, indeed probably thousands of very brave people. Ludomir Marczak, mentioned above, was shot in Pawiak prison in March 1944. In fact, between September 1942 and May 1944, some two hundred peasants were executed by the Germans for harboring Jews. In at least two instances, the inhabitants of an entire village were burned alive by the Germans for this crime. For in some places, in a hamlet called Osiny, for example, the peasants deliberately assumed collective responsibility and arranged that each should hide a Jewish girl for a certain period so that everyone would be guilty and no one could inform.

All in all, there was probably more done to help Jews than will ever be known, for of course we are less likely to hear about the helpers who were caught and murdered.

[4] These and subsequent individual stories are quoted from Tatiana Berenstein and Adam Rutkowski, *Assistance to the Jews in Poland*, Warsaw, 1963.

There is a man called Bartoszewski living in Warsaw who saved several dozen lives, and is one of those who has had a tree dedicated to him in Jerusalem. Even today he often feels desperate (he is a devout Catholic) at not having been able to do more. "But one in four wore a caftan," he says. "It takes at least two men successfully to hide one, and half of them hardly spoke Polish. How do you hide a man if he won't eat anything but kosher food?" How did one hide a child who might unwittingly blurt out some phrase in Yiddish in front of a German?

In a word, even the willing Pole was faced with almost insuperable difficulties. But in spite of the heroic examples we have mentioned, far too few were even willing. To be sure, German anti-Semitic propaganda fell on stony ground, for the Poles were only too clearly aware that they and the Jews were in the same terrible predicament. But the plain fact is that Poland stood by—in the main—and watched the murder of its Jews, if not with complacency, then at least in silence. It is easy at this distance in space and time to say that the Polish Jew needed a nation of giants for helpers and was fobbed off with mediocrities. But I suspect that the average intelligent Pole would admit that this is true.

Last of all, it must be admitted, if only in the interests of historical accuracy, that the Jewish record in this awful business left much to be desired too. Yet even here one must not generalize. Much has been written about the fact that six million victims went to their deaths like sheep. There were of course some who acted differently.

There was the immortal Dr. Korczak who of his own free will accompanied the orphans who trusted him into the gas chambers lest if they be left alone they be too afraid. There were men and women in that terrible spring of 1943 who, when only a remnant of about fifty thousand able-bodied young people was left alive in the ghetto, fought their hopeless and heroic uprising and sold those lives as dearly as they were able. Iccak Wittenberg was one such, or the beautiful Fruma Plot-nicka who died at Bedzin, or many others, some of them unknown, all unsung in Bialystok. There were some like "Znachor" in Lublin or Cywia Lubetkin in Warsaw or "Chytry" in Radom who escaped and fought and sur-vived in the partisan armies. And if most others lined up mute and unresisting to enter the transports, we must remember that hardly any of them knew what was to come—hardly anyone believed the Germans to be as savage as indeed they were.

Even so, SS General Jürgen Stroop who commanded the liquidation of the ghetto was puzzled when women with children in their arms leaped from the upper floors of burning buildings. "One has found throughout," he says, "that both the Jews and the bandits, in spite of the dangers of the conflagration, preferred to return into the flames rather than fall into our hands."[5]

*De mortuis nil nisi bonum*, and indeed one feels a sense

----

[5] Stroop's report to General Krüger in Cracow. Jürgen Stroop was captured after the end of the war, brought to trial in Warsaw, and subsequently hanged.

of guilt whenever one is critical of the dead, always in one's imagination freshly dying. But it would be wrong too to varnish plain facts with emotion.

What was deplorable was the almost complete lack in far too many of the doomed Jews of any sense of unity or cooperation. Read Alexander Donat who was there and who tells us how thousands joined the Jewish police and helped control and even to choose victims in the fruitless hope of saving their own skins.[6]

Or talk, as this observer has done, to survivors, in one case to a man who worked for two years in the ghetto. Probably it was the Germans he worked for, and that is why he has asked to remain anonymous. He and everyone else who lived through those days agrees that the rich ate; the poor starved and died in full view of any passer-by in the street. Even in the ghetto and in the midst of war, money bought comfort. For money German soldiers could be found to bring in cattle to be slaughtered by kosher butchers. For money, even though you lived in the ghetto, you could buy champagne and good French wine.

One story sticks in the mind—of an old Jew who

[6] Alexander Donat, *The Holocaust Kingdom*, Holt, Rinehart, and Winston, New York, 1965. Donat is the pseudonym of Michal Berg, who owned (it must be said) a rather shabby little paper called *Ostatnie Wiadomosci* in Warsaw before the war. His chief complaint against the Poles is that whereas they hid and thus saved his child, they turned the boy into an anti-Semite in the process. It seems to this writer logical that if one wished to save a small Jewish boy in that insane world, one had to wipe out any consciousness in him of being Jewish, or else he would almost inevitably betray both his rescuers and himself.

crawled along Mila Street on a winter afternoon until he came to a cellar window where a bowl of soup was set to advertise a restaurant. For some minutes he lay there, feebly sniffing the hot, good smell, until suddenly able to bear it no longer, he collected the last of his strength and stumbled down the steps into the basement out of sight. But almost immediately he came hurtling out again with a stream of Yiddish curses being shouted after him up from the dark doorway. According to the witness, who was working in a factory across the road, he lay there on the pavement for the rest of the short daylight. By nightfall he was dead and the paid Jewish scavengers carried him away.

Even in concentration camps the rich sold jewelry for food and jobs in dry, warm places. The poor rotted and found generosity nowhere, not even in those they had thought friends. A dozen or more witnesses—Jews and Christians alike—have described to this writer how mothers at selection points sometimes denied their own children, for children were a ticket to the gas chambers.

God knows if any of us, unthreatened as we are, would have acted differently. But it is painful to write about people like animals in slaughterhouses. One's sense of human dignity is offended. For the self-abasement, the degradation did not even help. They all died anyway, those who had survived typhus and starvation. Rich and poor, young, old, whatever they were, they all died the sudden, suffocating, bestial deaths of Treblinka, Majdanek, Sachsenhausen, Belzec, Auschwitz, Sobibor,

Mauthausen, Dachau, Buchenwald, Ravensbrück, Belsen, and many other places. One has seen their photographs as they stood there, stripped naked, actually waiting to be gassed, and in their eyes neither despair nor fear, but actually hope—hope that if they kept doing as they were told they would be allowed to survive after all.

Near Cracow the sky stank of burning flesh so that even the troops complained. Near Gdansk they made soap out of the bodies. From Lublin came hair for the inner linings of men's jackets, and for seats in railway carriages in which perhaps many honest Germans are riding even today.

And there was nothing human about what was done to them, nothing heroic or larger than life about what they suffered, nothing individual or proud. Once in a dog's age some woman would begin screaming uncontrollably, and lest she infect the rest they would simply hustle her round the corner of the gas chamber and give her a low-caliber bullet at the base of the brain. No more. All over in seconds. But even now, a generation afterward, people ask you to pick up a handful of earth in a vast field near Brzezinka—anywhere you like—and you do and find it speckled with a multitude of all but unrecognizable slivers of what they tell you is gray, human bone.

# 3. The Camps—Zamosc

In the middle years of the war Britain, America, and the Soviet Union fought for victory. Western Europe held on in the darkness and waited for daybreak and deliverance. Poland struggled in the almost desperate hope of not being annihilated before daybreak and deliverance came.

All secondary schools and universities had of course been closed, for Poles were supposed to be subhuman, and thus not in need of education. So in every town in the country schools began to be organized underground. As early as the sixth of November 1939, the Nazis had made plain that their plan for Poland was to be different from that for the west—not only in degree, but in kind. For on that afternoon a hundred and eighty-three professors of the University of Cracow were called to a meeting, supposedly to discuss how the university was to be run under German occupation. But no sooner had the meeting been opened than troops broke in, had the whole assemblage arrested, and deported *en masse* to Germany, where most of them were locked up in Sachsenhausen.

In spite of such oppression, the work of the universities went on—in basements, in private apartments, sometimes out in the villages. Courses were organized. Books were requisitioned and duplicated, examinations were set and even degrees conferred by the appropriate authorities.

Not only this. There were even underground theaters where Polish plays could be performed. Under Wilhelm II there had at least been one small Polish theater allowed (although only in a back street) in Poznan. Under Adolf Hitler, there was none. It is interesting to learn that the present Cardinal, former Archbishop Wojtyla of Cracow was a worker in a soda factory in those days, and had not even been ordained. But as a young man he had already discovered two of his passions—for acting and for mountaineering and, there being no reason to climb mountains, he had worked at underground theatricals instead. As a matter of fact, even today he has all the liveliness of an actor, and in his walk, indeed in his carriage, bears a striking resemblance to Sir Lawrence Olivier.

In Warsaw, of course, as all over the country, there were clandestine newspapers by the score. In fact, over a period of about five years some nine hundred different publications appeared at one time or another. One solitary Polish daily was printed under German auspices, the *Nowy Kurier Warszawski*, and a weekly, *Fala* (*The Wave*), which had a nose for pornography and not much else.

But the *Biuletyn Informacyjny*, its news gleaned largely from the BBC, was far more widely read, or *Trybuna Walności*, or *Wola Ludu*, or *Warszawianka*. There are stories far too numerous to retell of how presses were smuggled piece by piece into private houses and there assembled, how ink was found in sufficient quantities, and paper. Then the actual work of writing and printing had to be done—not only in secrecy, but in silence, with German police walking by outside the windows every ten or fifteen minutes. Finally, having printed your paper, you were faced with the even more dangerous job of distributing it.

For some reason, girls were generally the couriers. They would collect their bundles and drift across the city, each with a dozen or so copies wadded under her coat. These would be left, two or three at a time, with contacts at various cafes. And from there in turn they would be passed to customers who would hand them on until an edition, sometimes of no more than a few hundred copies, would be read by as many as thirty or forty thousand people.

Thus far the tidy facts, like the scenario of a film about heroes. The day-by-day drudgery and fear are something less easy to describe to one who was not there. Thus the Captain of a Polish vessel, a man called Draczkowski, and I sat at breakfast one morning in the saloon of his ship, *Jaslo*. He was far too young to have fought in the war.

"You ask how long before Poles will forget the occupation," he said. "Well, my father worked on an underground newspaper. I suppose you would not have heard of it—*Biuletyn Informacyjny* in Warsaw."

He gazed out at the misty Baltic through the porthole. "One night the Germans came at about two o'clock. They didn't knock. No, they broke down the door, broke up everything in the flat, and took my father away."

Again, silence. "Three days later he came back," the Captain said after a while. "His face was a mass of blood. He had no teeth, and it was years before he could hear again."

At last he looked up. "You ask how long." The voice was quiet, calm, conversational. "If I met the German who did that to my father just for writing the truth, I could kill him—today—with a knife."

This was in the spring of 1968.

All during the war there was of course regular radio contact with the outside world. Even the post got out (mostly through Sweden and Rumania), and couriers made their not-too-irregular runs to London and back. In July 1943, on the night General Sikorski died, it was in the company of one such courier, Bombardier Gralewski,[1] and it is a measure of the difficulties men

[1] David Irving, *op. cit.*

like him faced when we read that Gralewski had taken four and a half months to walk across Europe to Gibraltar.

By means of such couriers the facts about German death camps were first made public in the west. Prisoner David Szmulewski actually took photographs in Auschwitz of naked women being herded to the gas chambers, and these pictures were smuggled out through the gates. As early as November 1942, a courier got through to London from the Warsaw ghetto. But in those days the west was far too preoccupied with its own problems to worry about Poland's.

And yet even today in Poland these problems and these memories are still very much alive. It is not uncommon at all to meet people with numbers tattooed on their forearms. In the camps as many Christians died as Jews.[2] There are many stories one hears from survivors as vivid as though they had happened yesterday, and to walk through those places even now and see with one's own eyes things about which one has only read is to disturb all one's preconceptions about reality or the essential reasonableness of one's own or any other society.

Or to look at Majdanek first, as this writer did, before Auschwitz or Treblinka, is to think of it ever afterward

[2] This statement will of course be challenged and indeed it is almost impossible to determine whether or not it is entirely accurate. Certain camps, Treblinka for example, had almost nothing but Jewish prisoners. Auschwitz, at least in the early years, had a predominently non-Jewish population. Later the ratios changed. But all in all, some three million *Polish* Jews were killed and about the same number of Polish Christians. The exact figures will never be known.

as the worst; the vast, sloping plain with rectangular wooden barracks like parallel dominoes, the double row of barbed wire fencing and the watchtowers. To imagine the heat of summer with no water to be found, or snowdrifts blowing across that unbroken field with no warmth or shelter to be bought, one's food below the level of subsistence, one's clothing ragged and crusted with blood or excrement from some former owner, oneself parched or shivering, hopeless, lousy, and bewildered, waiting for the blow one dare not imagine at the back of the head—to picture all this is to get a notion what the far more complicated reality must have been like.

During 1941 the Germans decided to build a *cordon sanitaire* of Germanic settlers between the Reich and the Slav wilderness, so down in southeastern Poland in the region of Zamosc (temporarily renamed Himmlerstadt) they began clearing farmers out of their villages and locking them into a camp in Zamosc itself. Some two hundred and ninety-two villages were thus emptied of Poles (a village is any place containing fifty houses), and their inhabitants put into one of four categories.

The first was people of German extraction. The second was Poles fit to be put to work. The third was useless Poles, i.e., the old, the sick, the children. The fourth was composed of untouchables—gypsies and Jews.

It was all done quite methodically. At two or three o'clock in the morning a village would be surrounded and everyone called out into the market square. There they would be told they were going to be resettled and had twenty minutes to get dressed. Horses and carts (the long, narrow Polish carts with sloping sides) would already have been requisitioned, and when the twenty minutes were up, people would be herded into these carts, families all together, carrying whatever they had been able to pick up in the time allowed.

The only hope of escape, survivors say today, was at the start. Run for the wood and hope your guards could not see clearly enough in the dark to shoot you down. For as soon as the carts were in motion the motorcyclists and the troops marching alongside made flight quite out of the question. Into Zamosc by dawn, and there children would be taken from their parents and the great work begun of separating people into the appropriate categories.

Some families, of course, had already moved away to the forests and joined partisan bands. And incidentally, the Germans have used this fact as an excuse for the whole "Zamosc operation." Others (and many of these have survived) spent every night in the forest for years and only came back to the villages during daylight to work. For the Germans, being a methodical people, never made their arrests except in the dead of night. By the summer of 1942 there were skirmishes with these fugitives that lasted all day. By 1943 the Nazis had to bring in a whole Wehrmacht division to put down what they called the Zamosc uprising. The partisans blew bridges and derailed trains bound for the Russian front. In reprisal the Germans cleared more villages and turned them into little fortresses manned by armed German settlers.

Back in the Zamosc camp people died in their hundreds of disease and starvation. So the German authorities decided to show an unaccustomed mercy to some who were after all neither combatants nor Jews. They made up their minds to save children who were blond, blue-eyed, and young enough to forget their antecedents. On the twenty-seventh of November 1943, these began to be taken away from their parents and sent off to Germany for adoption.

In the meantime, of course, German troops were also trying to turn a penny here and there out of misfortune. There are half a dozen instances recorded of soldiers who sold children for as little as five or ten zlotys (a dollar or so) to families willing to pay that small stipend to rescue them.

As for the others—those with brown eyes—if they were twelve years and under, they stayed in Zamosc to starve. If they were at least thirteen they were shipped to Majdanek or Auschwitz where, on average, they survived about four months.

At Auschwitz, at least in the early years, the Germans kept records. Thus Krystyna Trzesniewska from Zamosc is listed as having been admitted to the camp on the thirteenth of December 1942. According to meteorological records in Cracow, it was a clear, cold, windy day. In the morning the temperature was just below freezing, in the afternoon, just above.

In Auschwitz in block 26 she had her head cropped, was stripped and marched naked across a muddy patch of earth into the bathhouse, showered and then, in spite of the fact that it was December, ordered out again, still naked, into the open where she lined up to be given prison clothing—a used shirt and pair of drawers, a striped cotton uniform that might or might not fit, and a pair of wooden clogs. These latter, she would eventually discover, always came off when she tried to walk in slush or mud, so like most of the girls and women she probably got into the habit of carrying them and going barefoot.

Having now been more or less clothed, Krystyna went to be tattooed with a number (in this case, 27,129) on her left forearm, and photographed—full face, profile, and half profile.

What block they put her in I have not been able to discover, or what work she did. If she had the strength to fight for her regular meals, she received a pint of black ersatz coffee for breakfast, a bowl of potato or turnip soup at noon, and for supper, imitation coffee again, a fistful of bread, and just under an ounce of sausage.

On this diet Krystyna survived until the eighteenth of May 1943. I have not been able to discover what the Germans listed as the cause of her death. For formal death certificates were written out too, by men like Dr.

Kremer, Professor of Anatomy at the University of Münster, or Dr. Hirt, also an anatomist, of Strasbourg, or Dr. Walter Capesius, head of the SS pharmacy, who was not brought to trial until 1964, or Josef Klehr, who from 1941 until 1943 murdered groups of prisoners with phenol injections. At *his* trial, incidentally, he admitted to having killed two hundred and fifty or three hundred people (the prosecution thought the true figure to be nearer fifteen thousand) and asked that the statute of limitations be applied. For after all, he had only acted under orders (thus it could surely be no more than manslaughter) and anyway it had happened years before. It was only in 1964, he said, that he had finally begun to understand what Auschwitz was all about.

There were various so-called "causes of death." "General debility" was one. That meant starvation. "Infection of the lungs" was to be understood as death by gassing. "Cerebral hemorrhage" was a bullet in the brain. I am inclined to believe Krystyna Trzesniewska probably died of "heart weakness." This meant she contracted typhus, diarrhea, or tuberculosis, as large numbers of the children did—was removed to block 28 (later block 20), stripped naked again, and after a short wait in a crowded room, sent into an adjoining chamber where she was dispatched by an injection of 30 per cent phenol through an enormous syringe directly into the heart. SS doctors found that by taking "patients" one by one and thus avoiding foreknowledge and the possibility of hysterical scenes, each man could destroy about thirty an hour in this way.

In the whole of the Zamosc operation about 110,000 people were either killed or deported. The Germans claim that it was only the SS that did these things. Survivors in Zamosc are emphatic in insisting that they were done by regular army units too. Those deported were of all ages, of many, many families. About 30,000 of them were children. Their names are largely unrecorded or forgotten. Of that thirty thousand, Krystyna Trzesniewska was one.

The German nation—taken as a whole—was no doubt secretly shocked and ashamed when it learned of some of the worse crimes committed by Germans in the name of Germany. And so much murder was done, that by comparison to strip a thirteen-year-old Polish girl naked and make her stand in a crowded field waiting to be branded would hardly be considered a crime worth remembering. The fact that it would not be so considered is a measure of the degradation visited by Germany on the Poles. One understands death in war, slaughter, horror, murder perhaps, but one does not forgive humiliation. That is why the Poles dread and loathe Germans with an intensity it will take generations to overcome.

Majdanek and Treblinka were death camps largely for Jews. Auschwitz was originally intended chiefly for Poles. Jozef Cyrankiewicz, the present Polish Prime Minister, was an inmate of block 25. Tomasz Sobanski, who works in Warsaw today, was another, and he not only survived in Auschwitz for three whole years; at the end of that time he actually escaped.

Sobanski is a nervous, handsome, likeable man in his early forties, with brilliant blue eyes, and he tells you his story with the words popping out like bullets from a muted machine gun. The underground slipped him out of Auschwitz on condition that he come back into the district to help. It had been a matter of exquisite planning—getting off on a work party that had an SS man in charge so that no Pole could be blamed (and shot) for his disappearance. Then the hiding in a cellarage for two days and nights, being dragged out by confederates when the coast was clear, and finally being transported into hiding in Cracow while his hair grew and his tattooed number could be removed.

And then the false papers, the certification that he worked as a miner, the going out at night in a stolen SS uniform, and at last the innumerable escapades, each far more dangerous than normal combat. On one occasion he ordered an SS escort to hand over its prisoners to him, actually gave the Germans a receipt, and marched the Poles off out of captivity. On another he accompanied two SS officers into an ambush, at the proper moment pulled a pistol and disarmed them.

"A moment before, they'd been bragging. Then their mouths fell open in horror and they were down in the mud, sobbing and kissing my boots." A pause for thought. He takes a sip of vodka. "It's very difficult indeed to blow out a man's brains when he is kissing your boots."

Certain phrases of Sobanski's stick in the mind by reason of the echoes they evoke—and the overtones.

"In Auschwitz it was a matter of fight or die. God knows it was hard, but in a way you were master of your fate.

"When a thousand women come out of the cattle trucks in which they've been locked for three or four days, they are in fact hardly human. They stink, and some of them have blood on their legs because of course they haven't been able to wash.

"I never saw Höss (the camp commandant) strike a man. But his little daughter did. She'd canter round on horseback, laughing and hitting prisoners with her riding crop."

According to Sobanski, the London-led AK sent in a man by parachute to blow a hole in the wire. "But it would never have worked," he says. "A few hundred might have got free, but for the others in that open countryside it would have been a massacre."

Sobanski's mother, father, and brother were all dead by the time of his arrest, killed by the Germans. He thinks that perhaps this made it easier for him to go on. He had no responsibilities.

Or, in another connection, "You talk about your six million murdered," he says, "but you tend to forget the wounded." Today, twenty-five years after it all happened, he cannot bear for anyone to walk behind him in the street. He steps aside and lets them pass. Even a tram conductor coming toward him in uniform makes the palms of his hands sweat. He laughs deprecatingly.

"One cannot be logical about these things," he says. "I have a wife who's an excellent housekeeper, but every night on my way home I buy a loaf of bread. I know perfectly well there's bread in the kitchen. She has never failed to remember the bread." He shrugs and glances over at one apologetically. "But I can't help it. I still buy bread."

Certain things bewilder him. He was called as a witness at the trial of various SS men in Frankfurt. "There was one I had known well," he says. "I'd been there. With my own eyes I had seen him shoot women in the back of the head. But he was acquitted by reason of lack of evidence."

What makes him saddest of all is that nothing has been learned. As we talked that afternoon in Warsaw, America was making Vietnam the same murderous desert that Germany had made of Poland a generation before. At this he shrugged too. "It would be ridiculous to compare Johnson and Hitler," he murmured. "But they did have one thing in common. Each was stubborn because he knew he was right."

I was given an abrupt confirmation that some people, at least, have learned nothing at all. I walked round Majdanek with a former prisoner all one terrible morning, and at the sight of the exhibits, the piles of shoes, the hair, the tiny case with three smashed dolls, found it

[ 47 ]

difficult to control my voice and conduct a normal conversation.

I asked my companion if German tourists ever visited the place.

"Oh, yes," was the answer. "Often."

"And how do they react?"

"React?" the man asked sharply, and turned. "They don't react. Ninety per cent of them tell me it's Polish propaganda."

# 4. The Tide Turns

In 1943 the tide finally turned—with Stalingrad, North Africa, the invasion of Sicily. And with fresh hope, the Poles, too, began to go over to the offensive. Not only were there partisans in the Zamosc region. Near Lublin too, and Kielce, armed detachments were tying down more and more German troops. And in Warsaw there were almost daily attacks on members of the occupying forces.

The history of Communism, indeed of left-wing revolutionary movements in Eastern Europe, is so complex, so full of schismatics and violence, of hyperbole trying to make precise the imprecise and to denigrate theories an impartial observer would find it difficult to distinguish from the denigrator's, that to set it down fairly would be far beyond the scope of this book. And of course, as in the writings of the early Church fathers, dogma is so much more important than objective fact, what ought to be true so often preferred to what is, that one must walk through Communist accounts, even of recent events, as though through a minefield.

Novalis said that "conviction gains infinitely once another soul believes in it," and revolutionists press more eagerly than the rest of us for conviction. In their canon, words are not used for their meanings so much as for their utility, and to call a man "a lackey of the imperialists," or to ascribe to an opponent the most complex and diabolical motives is simpler and perhaps more effective than to discuss his opinions rationally.

Polish Socialists, like any others, wear their history with a difference, but in one respect they are unique. Polish resistance during the war was largely that of the AK, led by the exiled government in London. The AK were more numerous, better organized, and, while not better armed, far more effective than their Communist counterparts. And although the present Polish government pays lip service to the dogma that most resistance to the Nazis was Communist inspired, although the twenty-second of July when the Lublin government was formed is a national holiday and the first of August when Warsaw rose against the Germans is not, modern Polish accounts of the war do concede that the so-called London reactionaries were a major force in the country's liberation. No other Socialist government has ever made such an admission. In passing, let it be noted too that Poland is almost unique in the Eastern bloc in not having named a city after one of its heroes. Perhaps the

Polish awareness of the perpetuity of change prevented it—or the Polish sense of humor.

In any event, as the Russian army began moving west and the Anglo-American forces landed—first in Italy and then on the coast of France—Polish resistance grew too until it became a serious danger and at one moment even threatened to cut off the Germans' retreat into the Reich.

Fighting in Warsaw had begun as a series of attacks and retaliations. Thus in October 1942 the Germans publicly executed fifty members of the underground. Eight days later a group of Polish youths threw hand grenades into the Cafe Club at the corner of Nowy Swiat and Jerozolimskie (it was reserved for Nazi officers). That same night they attacked the Mitropa restaurant and the printing plant of the German-controlled *Nowy Kurier Warszawski,* and in the course of these operations killed some thirty-one Germans.

For months afterward there were mass arrests, house-to-house searches all over the city, and people were sent either to Auschwitz, Majdanek, or the terrible Pawiak prison in Warsaw itself.

Maria Bankowska, journalist and wife of a former Polish correspondent in London, spent some time in Pawiak. She had broken her leg, been picked up quite by chance at her dressmaker's, and the Germans suspected her of having come in by parachute. As so many other Poles have done, she said to this writer, "You weren't there, but *I saw it.* No one who didn't see with his own eyes can ever understand what happened." She was kept for several months in a cell with thirty other women, and almost daily, people were taken out to a room at the end of the corridor to be shot.

"I saw and heard it myself," she insists. "It would be the turn of some woman with a baby in her arms. 'Shoot me first,' she would beg. But almost invariably they would shoot the child first. The only possible explanation is that it gave them pleasure."

It is like the story of Aleksander Kulisiewicz who spent five years in Sachsenhausen.[1] He was (and is) a singer, and whiled away many evenings in prison with Jean-Louis Barrault and others, organizing secret performances of poetry and music. Of course he took pleasure in these activities, and this so annoyed the chief camp doctor, Heinz Baumkotter, that he gave Kulisiewicz three separate injections of diphtheria in an attempt to destroy his voice.

In May 1943, six hundred political prisoners from Pawiak were executed in the ruins of the ghetto. A month later the Gestapo arrested Lt. General Rowecki, Commander-in-Chief of the Home Army. A fortnight after that the Communist People's Guard[2] struck back with grenades at a column of Sturmabteilungen marching down the Aleje Ujazdowskie. Thirty Germans were killed.

Sometimes, according to the Poles, even assassination

[1] See his story in *The Times*, November 9, 1967.
[2] It was not called People's Army until 1944.

had its humorous side. A German officer was killed in the street by a man who had pulled a submachine gun out of a violin case. For weeks afterward anyone carrying a violin case was forced to open it for inspection. So people who had never played the violin in their lives took to carrying one simply to annoy.

These attacks were only the beginning, the first faint rumbling of the revolt that was to break out a whole year afterward. In any event, German patrols, instead of being carried out by two or three men at a time, grew to platoon strength and were armed with automatic weapons. Walkie-talkie radios were brought in, and by their help armored vehicles turned up with astonishing speed whenever they were needed.

Sometimes there would be days—even weeks—of quiet. Then there would come a Home Army attack out of the blue, or a *lapanka*, and people would sit at the bridge tables in their cafes, listening over the slap of the cards and the chatter of their companions for sounds from out in the streets.

In Mazowiecka Street, writers and painters congregated in the *Ziemianska*, or Dugout, run by a man called Skonski and his partner, Albrecht, who weighed almost three hundred pounds and who could hardly walk. Or they went to *Znachor* in Boduena Street, where everyone knew everyone else and the latest news (of the fronts, of the Home Army) passed softly from mouth to mouth.

A woman who has asked to remain nameless tells a

bizarre and frightening story about those days. She was only a child—eleven or twelve years old—but deeply in love with her cousin, a boy of eighteen who was a member of the underground. Whenever he came home from a meeting or some exploit she sat beside him, held onto his arm, hung on his every word.

"It is no idle phrase," she says today. "I was aware of the war and utterly aware of all our dangers. I would quite literally have died for him. I often thought of it."

Then one night news was brought them that he had been arrested by the Gestapo. She said nothing, did nothing, but felt her whole body frozen while she listened to the grown-ups whispering about how to hide or deny any possible connection they had had with him. She neither ate nor slept, but in her imagination felt him being tortured. A day or so afterward they were sent word that he had been executed.

She had never read the *Iliad*—had never heard of Hector's body—but she knew without any question what ought to be done. It was a cool April evening. She said not a word to anyone in the family, but put on her coat, a small fur hat that she wore, and walked round to the local Gestapo office.

"I want you to give me my cousin's body," she said. "I want to bury him."

What talk passed between her and the German officers she did not tell me. But the upshot of it was that at last they offered her the body for 10,000 zlotys (perhaps $500). This is a sizable sum today. In 1944 it would have amounted to an average workman's wages for well over a year and a half.

So back home she went to her family, and told them. They were terrified at what she had done, but even more terrified at the thought of returning with her to the Gestapo.

Such was her intensity, however, that they were left with no choice. They gave her 10,000 zlotys, and off she went again and handed it over. Together she and a Gestapo officer went to the graveyard with the body and saw it buried.

"I made him pull the sheet back off the face," she said, "to prove they had given me the right man."

It must have been a frightening time for the Germans themselves. Not many even of the whores would talk to them—or if one did, not too long afterward she would be seized and her head would be shaved by two or three men in the middle of the night and she never the wiser as to who her attackers had been.

Colonel Netzer (formerly of the Home Army) tells how he stood waiting for a tram one night in Marszalkowska. Trams ran as twin carriages, joined one to the other. The first was for Germans, the second for Poles.

In front of him that night stood two German officers in heavy fur collars, with revolvers strapped round their waists. Along came two young Polish girls, also in furs. A quick look round to make certain there were no sentries in sight. Then out came razor blades. In two or three strokes they had severed the Germans' belts. Revolvers, holsters and all disappeared into their own muffs. Half a dozen Poles who saw the operation crowded round to shield them. Then, with the officers not having felt a thing, they sauntered off. Behind them, two boys strolling as though aimlessly, hands in their pockets, eyes darting watchfully from side to side.

Out in the countryside the most malignant Gestapo officers were often taken prisoner and killed. It happened in Warsaw too, and one Warsovian who never had anything to do with the resistance witnessed such an execution quite by accident. He was a tram driver on the number 25 that ran down Grojecka, and one evening just before curfew he had a solitary SS officer riding in the first carriage directly behind him.

In the middle of a block a Pole leaped aboard in the dusk. The driver turned round in astonishment to see a compatriot in the place reserved for Germans, and was just in time to see the man holding a pistol in the officer's back.

Loud and clear the voice came. "Gruppenführer Schramm [or some such name], by a decree of the court of the Polish underground, you have been sentenced to death." A bit of paper was thrust into the German's pocket; there was the muted crack of a pistol shot, and before the driver was really aware of what had happened, the German had crumpled to the floor and his unknown executioner had leaped off and disappeared into the dark.

Sometimes partisans acted with a slightly macabre sense of humor. The Holy Cross prison near Kielce held some twelve thousand Russian prisoners of war who had been dying like maggots on potato soup and half a pound of bread a day. In the course of time about a hundred and fifty managed to escape and reach the Gwardia Ludowa. The rest simply rotted away, and indeed, of all that twelve thousand—including those who escaped—just one man managed to survive the war.

This was a certain Sergyei Aleksyevitch Kotov, and he must be a man of almost incredible endurance and ingenuity. He fled over the wall one winter night in 1941 by tying his puttees into a rope. He weighed just seventy-nine pounds. He was unarmed, in a frozen, unfamiliar countryside, spoke not a word of Polish, and could hardly walk. Two peasants found him, dragged him into a barn, and for two weeks he lay there in the straw, gasping with pneumonia and sipping the occasional bowl of soup they were able to bring him.

But Kotov wasn't the sort who died easily. He went to work as a farm laborer to regain his strength. Then he joined a partisan group, quickly became a leader, and went on foray after foray until even the Germans developed a certain respect for him. Then, one night in January 1943, he exacted a peculiarly Russian revenge for his previous humiliations.

One of the more prosperous farmers in the neighborhood had fled from the Red Army at the time of the revolution, and was naturally accepted by the Germans as a friend. In fact, he often entertained them in his house.

But Kotov went to see him one day and somehow or other talked him round. Were they not both Russians? Did they not speak a common language? Did they not love Pushkin? In a word, he got a promise that the farmer would cooperate. And sure enough, a few days later Kotov was sent word that twenty German officers would be at the farm that night for supper.

It must have been an evening that whoever among them is alive can still remember. Suddenly in the midst of the meal the lights went out. And before they knew which way to turn, Kotov and his men had swarmed in at the doors and windows and backed them against the wall at pistol point. First their weapons—slung into a pile in the corner. Then their uniforms—under protest this time, campaign ribbons, jackboots, and all.

And when they finally stood there in long, woolen underwear, the worst indignity of the lot.

"Is there any vodka in the house?" Kotov cried out.

There was. So at gunpoint the Germans drank a stiff vodka each to Poland and liberty. And when they had downed that, another—a third, a fourth, a fifth. Within twenty minutes they were blear-eyed and hardly able to stand on their feet. It was then Kotov ordered them out into their cars—and twenty disarmed, drunk, and half-naked officers drove back to headquarters with a terrible set of explanations to make to their Colonel.

And Kotov? He and his men slipped out into the wood again, and from there back to their separate villages. As the old partisan song had it, they had sallied out to steal weapons for Poland, heard their own marching footsteps loud between the houses, and the wind kept making a song about them as they marched.

Kotov's war was luckier than many. He and his group were encircled at last one autumn evening, and after a twelve-hour battle he was captured, badly wounded. The Gestapo took him to Radom for questioning, then sent him to Dachau for execution. But, bureaucrats to the last, at the very door to the gas chamber, certain Germans dragged him out of the queue. The number on his arm did not correspond to the one on file. So he was spared, sent to Mauthausen, and at last liberated by the Americans at the very end of the war.

Back in Warsaw, the Communist People's Guard (now grown into the People's Army) made at least two offers to join forces with the Home Army, but the government in exile turned these down, fearing of course that partnership would lead to a takeover, particularly if, as now seemed likely, Poland were to be liberated by the Red Army and not by the British and Americans coming in from the west.

And so these two groups continued to fight Germans under separate commands and, above all, with different strategies in mind. The goal of the People's Army (or AL) was to cause confusion behind the German lines and thus facilitate the westward thrust of the Soviet forces when they came. The purpose of the Home Army (or AK) was to spread its area of influence, gradually, as German power weakened, to take over the cities, and to greet the Red Army when it came, not as liberators, but as guests in an organized Polish state. This was something the Communists could never have done. To control an area of Poland as the AK did would for the AL have been quite impossible, because to be blunt about it, the Communists were far too unpopular. The Russian-German pact that had enabled Hitler to start his war, the Russian murder of Polish officers in Katyn forest, and Stalin's well-known and ruthless cynicism simply put the seal to an enmity that had lasted well over three hundred years.

On the first of February 1944, the underground pulled off its greatest coup, the assassination in the open Aleje Ujazdowskie of General Kutschera, commander of the German security forces for the Warsaw district.

The reprisals were terrible, but from then on no German's life was safe, not even in Warsaw, hundreds of miles behind the front. In June the Russians, joined now by the First Polish Army (trained on Russian soil) reached the Bug and crossed it into present-day Polish territory. Chelm and Lublin were liberated, and the first task of the troops who entered Lublin was to bury the corpses of three hundred Polish prisoners whom the Germans had murdered before their own departure. A man who was there tells me the job had to be done in gas masks.

On the twenty-second of June, a government largely Communist, but including token representation from other parties, was formed in Lublin. London took note.

The Red Army reached the Vistula south of Warsaw, and suddenly London realized they were in danger of losing their cause by default.

Now there had long been Home Army plans for a nationwide revolt—the so-called *burza*—when the time came, and for that purpose arms had been distributed— and dropped by the RAF—to a large number of groups all over the country. But with no adequate liaison and no real knowledge in London of the exact situation in Poland, on the twenty-fifth of July a wireless order was sent to prepare for action in Warsaw alone. The next day the order was revoked.

By that time (so violent had been the Russian attack, so heavy the German casualties), a hundred and sixty Red Army divisions were driving westward, faced by only a tenth that number of Germans. On the twenty-third of July in Warsaw, Maria Bankowska had sat in her window on the sixth floor of a building overlooking Jerozolimskie and watched the German army fleeing westward. Across the river in Praga one could make out smoke rising into the still air, and down below her she could see damaged guns being towed, men marching without boots, wounded men limping along on sticks, men with horses and carts. "It was a positively Napoleonic retreat," she says, a whole beaten army streaming toward Berlin.

Off to the east across the Vistula they could hear gunfire. General Bor-Komorowski, by now in command of the Home Army in Warsaw, writes that "from the

28th of July we could hear the noise of battle on the outskirts. Soviet tanks were making deep inroads into the defenses of the German bridgehead. Places only ten miles outside Warsaw were already held by the Russians.[3]

According to him, on July twenty-ninth Moscow radio appealed to the people of Warsaw to rise, and promised them immediate support. This writer has found no record of any such broadcast, and authorities in Warsaw deny that it was ever made. What they do say is that there were Russian broadcasts asking Poland (as opposed to Warsaw alone) to rise, and that of course is an entirely different matter. In a word, in the light of Stalin's cabled advice to Churchill and Roosevelt that he either could or would not help a Warsaw rising, and the refusal of Red Army commanders in the field to allow the RAF to land for refueling behind their lines, it would seem probable that General Bor-Komorowski was mistaken.

In any case, he says[4] that it was only on the thirty-first when a Soviet communique announced the capture of the commander of the Seventy-third German division defending the bridgehead in Praga that he ordered the uprising to start on the following day.

[3] The General writes this in his introduction to Waclaw Zagorski's *Seventy Days*, Frederick Muller, London, 1957. But according to the evidence in Chapter 6 which follows, it is clear the Russians had got nowhere near so far. So when he talks of "a German bridgehead," or says that places only ten miles away were held by the Russians, he may be technically correct. There may have been isolated Russian units that close to the city. But in the main his argument sounds like special pleading.
[4] In his introduction to *Seventy Days. Ibid.*

But on the night of the twenty-sixth Maria Bankowska had been asleep in her shelter when she heard tanks rumbling overhead. Her first thought was that the Russians had arrived. She was mistaken. It was the Hermann Göring division headed east to reinforce General Vormann's wavering Ninth Army. The Germans were not nearly as badly beaten as the optimists supposed.

Although General Bor claims that no decision had been reached until the thirty-first, orders had already been sent out several days before to cut passages from cellar to cellar under the streets. Caches of arms had already been distributed, and in inner courtyards all over the city men had gathered, wearing red and white armbands.

The truth is the Polish High Command (both in London and in Warsaw) simply could not make up its mind. Attack, and it might be too early, and in any case, there had been no time to bring men and arms back in from the countryside. Wait, on the other hand, and the Communist Armia Ludowa (no doubt in collaboration with the Russians) might attack in their place and claim credit for liberating the city. Or the Red Army would come marching in by itself and simply fill the power vacuum left by the flight of the Germans.

But on the thirtieth or thirty-first of the month they realized the decision was no longer in their hands. The insurgents had already gathered and were far too exposed to retreat, for the Germans had begun erecting cement blockhouses on street corners and arming them with machine guns. German patrols had everywhere been heavily reinforced, and this alone would have made it impossible for Polish troops to be dispersed during the day, even if the authorities had wished to do so. At night, with a strict curfew in force, any Pole in the street would have been shot without warning.

So, decision or no, revolt was now inevitable, and nowhere can I remember a clearer exemplification of the Tolstoyan view of history. Men do not move events. Events have a way of moving by themselves. The Poles knew what was going to happen. The Germans knew it, and far off across the river the Russians undoubtedly knew it too.

In Warsaw itself—its population reduced now from almost 1,250,000 to under 900,000—there was food and ammunition for from seven to ten days. Somewhere between 20,000 and 40,000 men (the figures vary, depending upon the politics of the statistician), only about ten per cent of them adequately armed, stood ready. For we must remember that far from storing up further supplies in Warsaw, the AK had actually sent arms out of the city when a nationwide uprising was still considered feasible. Girls and women had been called up to organize soup kitchens, staff first aid stations, to act as telephonists, and—equally important—to serve as couriers through what everyone knew would be the rubble-filled streets when normal communications had broken down.

To be certain of success, there were several key points

that had to be taken whatever happened. The power station was one, and Jerozolimskie, the city's main artery running across from the Poniatowski Bridge, another. Third, fourth, fifth, and sixth in order of priority were Gestapo headquarters in Szucha, the Czech legation (a heavily armed strong point), the Sejm, or Parliament building (a German barracks), and the Post Office. They had all been fitted with bunkers. They were all bristling with armament.

Night fell at last on the thirty-first on that city, almost a third of whose people had already been killed. The air was hot and close. All over Warsaw families were carrying stocks of food down into the cellars. All over Warsaw, behind blackout curtains, men were making antitank bombs out of potassium chloride, sulphuric acid, and bottles of petrol. In the courtyards and cellars, in Czerniakow and Powisle, in Mokotow, Muranow, Wola, and Stare Miasto, the thousands upon thousands waited. Tomorrow they were going to take their revenge for five years of bitter humiliation. Tomorrow those thousands would show Germany and the world what kind of men Poles were.

The radio crackled with coded signals to and from Polish headquarters in London. Far off to the east across the river, the faint, perhaps only imagined flicker of Russian artillery. Along the riverbank itself, watched by German sentries, several hundred men were digging trenches to stave off a Soviet attack.

In all Poland's bloody history of struggle against its

invaders, no *powstanie*, no uprising had ever succeeded. But this time as it went to sleep, at least half the city was already in on the secret, that next day, on the first of August 1944, at five in the afternoon, they were going to start the greatest *powstanie* of them all.

# 5. Uprising in Warsaw

In Warsaw, Tuesday, the first of August, started like any other day. Trams rattled down the wide, interminable thoroughfares. People went to their shops and offices. Old women stood on street corners selling flowers, and here and there someone had trundled up one of the little handcarts from which he sold glasses of cold water and synthetic fruit juice.

Karol Zagorski, a banker with some twenty years' experience in the Far East, went off to work from his house in Chopina at the usual time. It was only a ten-minute walk down Krucza to the Narodowy Bank at the corner of Nowy Swiat and Jerozolimskie.

Several days before, he had heard rumors that an uprising was in the wind. That morning he heard it confirmed. Fighting was to start at five in the afternoon. So like any prudent man, he left work at two and went out to buy a stretcher, for his wife was ill and it occurred to him that if the struggle lasted more than two or three days she might have to be moved. Then he went home for his dinner, which Poles take in the middle of the afternoon.

At about four o'clock his mother-in-law went out from Chopina to the chemist in Mokotowska to have a prescription filled, but hours passed without any sign of her return. She had been trapped in the chemist's doorway by gunfire out of an adjoining building. As a matter of fact, she did not get back home until about nine o'clock that night. At one point Zagorski went down to look for her, but the porter of his building told him to stay indoors. It seemed they were throwing Molotov cocktails down at the corner and it was not really safe to show oneself.

The revolt actually started earlier than planned—up in Zoliborz in the northern part of the city, where at about half past one some boys who had not yet reached their posts were caught by the Germans trying to cross an open space with rifles in their hands. Firing broke out, of course. The boys ran for cover and began building a barricade.

Within half an hour—by midafternoon, that is—German blockhouses had been reinforced all over Warsaw, but the partisans wearing red and white armbands were already sallying out of their courtyards and taking over street after street, district after district. In those early hours, the Germans, still uncertain just how strong the insurgents were and how widespread the revolt was going to be, mostly held to their strong points and waited. So by early evening the Poles actually controlled huge areas of central Warsaw from Zoliborz and Stare Miasto in the north to Powisle, Mirow, and Wola in the center and Mokotow in the south. Red and white banners began appearing on the tops of buildings. The most heartening sight of all was an enormous Polish flag flying from the PKO building in Trzech Krzyzy. All over town a feeling of pride grew, of exultation, of fresh energy the like of which nobody had known for years.

For military purposes, Warsaw had been divided by the insurgents into five sectors—all under the command of the famous Colonel (later General) "Monter," Monter being the pseudonym of an old, regular army officer called Antoni Chrusciel. It was customary for underground fighters to use false names in order to protect relatives in the event of their capture.

At the start, he had opposing him two German divisions with tanks and aircraft. A few days later a third division was hurriedly brought in from Italy. And in addition to these there were large numbers of the gendarmerie shipped in from Poznan under SS Gruppenführer Lt. General Heinz Reinefarth.

According to Col. Netzer, who headed the "Kryska" group that fought so heroically far to the south in Czerniakow, the final orders for the uprising had come as early as the twenty-eighth of July, two days after

German reinforcements had entered the city, and by the end of the month mobilization had been far too generally observed to be canceled. Some of the men waited three whole days in the cellars and courtyards. It became difficult to feed them, much less keep them concealed, and even that early—speaking purely as a military man —he had had misgivings, for in his battalion only about one man in eight was armed. In fact, shortage of arms, not of food or courage, was their greatest difficulty during the entire nine weeks. Indeed, at one point he telephoned Col. Monter to plead for more rifles.

"Haven't your men got sticks and spades?" came the answer. "Haven't they hands? Don't they know where to find Germans? Well, tell them to go get guns from the Germans."

The first triumph was the capture of the Czech legation, guarded by an SS company two hundred strong. At five in the afternoon, twelve men led by a certain Major Ruczay ambushed the two guards at the entrance and stormed into the building. There they were cut off for hours from the outside world. In the confusion no one could find out what had become of them, until at about nine o'clock that night a girl crawled through to headquarters in Trzech Krzyzy to say that they had taken the first floor and were now attacking the second. Seventy Germans were eventually killed in the operation and a hundred taken prisoner. But even more important, all of their weapons were seized.

On the other hand, the attack on Gestapo headquarters in Szucha failed. So did that on the Sejm building. Four companies went into that onslaught, but very soon lost all their officers and had to retire toward the river. There they were cut off. Three days later (they had no wireless), when it became desperately necessary to send back news of their position, and when every possible way out of their cul de sac was found to be guarded, another girl courier stumbled on a brave and brilliant idea. She simply walked out toward the German lines with her hands in the air. No one fired, so when she thought she had got far enough to have a chance, she ducked her head between her shoulders and ran for it off between the buildings.

As Netzer says, eighty per cent of the men fought bravely, but the courage of the girls passed all understanding. Perhaps, he suggests, they lacked the experience to realize just how dangerous some of the things were that they did.

At any rate, those four companies from the attack on Szucha held out under their N.C.O.'s against half a German regiment until, after a solid week of beating off German attacks, they were ordered to get away to the south toward Czerniakow, where up until then there had been not even a headquarters, much less any organized resistance.

The power station was seized fairly early in the struggle but, this being a very important position, the Germans counterattacked and took it back. It changed hands during the course of the fighting several times until, during the last days the Nazis took it and held it to the end.

And so the long, long battle started. Waclaw Zagorski (not to be confused with the banker mentioned above) has written a book in diary form[1] which tells more or less what it was like to be there. I say more or less, simply because the author was never able to see more than his own small sector of the front. It is unquestionably an honest book. It is written from the point of view of one who believed (and still believes) that the London Poles were entirely in the right, and it sets down the day-to-day monotony of being dive bombed or attacked with mortar and cannon fire when all you have to fight back with are homemade grenades and Molotov cocktails.

I said before that the Poles, if they were to be successful, had to take certain key points. In most cases they failed, and the Germans held on, simply because the insurgents could do little against the enormous and ubiquitous fire power that the enemy was able to send against them. But nevertheless the partisans stood firm in what gradually even the most sanguine came to realize was a hopeless struggle. And they stood firm for three main reasons.

During the course of the revolt the Red Army reached Praga just across from the center of the city on the other side of the river. It was reasonably to be expected that they would renew their attack any day, cross

[1] Waclaw Zagorski, *Seventy Days*, Frederick Muller, London, 1957.

into Warsaw, and help turn the uprising into a rout of the German forces.

Second, the news from the western front was of one brilliant victory after another. Paris was liberated on the twenty-fifth of August, Brussels and Antwerp on the third and fourth of September. In four days British troops drove two hundred miles through the broken German positions and entered Holland. To their east, American tanks reached the Rhine near Aachen. In Italy, the famous Gothic line was broken. Whole German armies were being engulfed. Indeed, by the end of August the Germans had lost 500,000 men, as well as almost all their tanks, artillery, and transport.

"As far as I was concerned," General Rundstedt said a year afterward, "the war ended in September."[2] So to the Poles who of course heard most of their news through the BBC, it seemed not unreasonable to hope for a Nazi surrender no matter what the Russians might do.

And third, there was Lt. General Heinz Reinefarth (at the time of writing, still Mayor of Westerland on the island of Sylt). If what the Polish government says is true, and they present a very strong case indeed,[3] no man in his senses would ever have surrendered to troops under Reinefarth's command.

The facts seem to be as follows. On the first of August when the uprising broke out, Himmler was at the

[2] British War Office interrogation as quoted in Milton Shulman's *Defeat in the West*, New York, 1948.
[3] Kazimierz Leszczynski, *Heinz Reinefarth*, Wydawnictwo Zachodnie, Warsaw, 1961.

Führer's headquarters in East Prussia. According to a speech he made later in Jägerhöhe, he went at once to Hitler, who issued an order that Warsaw was to be razed to the ground. It is interesting to remember that the attempt on Hitler's life had been made only twelve days before. The Führer was still overwrought and desperate for revenge. It is difficult to find any other reason for an order that his troops destroy the only rail and road junctions immediately behind their own front lines.

Be that as it may, on the next day, the second of August, Himmler arrived in Poznan and gave an order to send divers police, Wehrmacht, and SS units there to Warsaw. On that same day he gave command of these units to Lt. General Heinz Reinefarth. Further, he ordered SS Oberführer Dirlewanger, at that time stationed with his Sturmbrigade at Olecko, to proceed also with all speed to Warsaw where he was to be "fully empowered and authorized to kill anybody he wished in accordance with his whim."[4]

The Dirlewanger brigade, composed of 860 men equipped with heavy machine guns and mine throwers, was duly transported by truck to Wola, the westernmost district of Warsaw. On the next day, August third, Reinefarth, too, reported at Ninth Army Headquarters in

[4] Testimony of Ernest Rode, Chief of Staff of the Korpsgruppe von dem Bach to Jerzy Sawicki, Polish prosecutor at Nuremberg. *Zburzenie Warszawy*, Katowice, 1946. This was in fact not so startling a directive as it might seem. From October 15, 1943 until June 1944, the Germans had already held seventy public executions in Warsaw and killed 5150 people.

Skierniewice, and on the fourth of August was already present in Wola at the head of his detachments. For Ninth Army command reported on August fourth at 23:15 hours on the strength of SS forces for the fight against the uprising, and stated that as of 22:00 hours, "The command over these forces lies in the hands of Major General [*sic*] of the Police Reinefarth, Higher SS and Police Leader in Poznan."[5] So on the fifth of August Heinz Reinefarth was the general in command against the Poles in Wola.

Wola is—and was—a poor working-class district of the city, and the first four days of the revolt had passed reasonably quietly there. But at about seven o'clock on the morning of the fifth, German troops launched an attack along Wolska Street toward the center of town. They totaled over three thousand men, supported by the guns of an armored train, tanks, and bombardment from the air. By afternoon the Germans had advanced the better part of a mile and had a large section of Wola under their control.

Next morning the captured area was cordoned off. People were driven out of their houses, herded into courtyards, parks, and factories like cattle into so many pens and shot down by machine gun fire—or else, if they were in an enclosed space, blown apart with grenades. In Sowinski Park alone that day more than a thousand

[5] Archives of the Central Commission for the Investigation of Nazi Crimes in Poland 1101/Z/. Vol. 7.

civilians, men, women, and children, were simply mown down. Some people were ordered to rip planks out of fences and hold them to their bodies as they were shot so that afterward they would burn more easily.

It is difficult to choose two or three from among the dozens of statements later made by people who miraculously survived. For example, one Janina Rozinska testified: "The people were fleeing in headlong panic. The SS men were hurrying them on along Wolska Street in the direction of the tramway depot in Mlynarska Street.

"Together with my children I found myself in the depot amidst a crowd of some two hundred persons . . . driven there both from the shelter of the Franaszek factory and from Wolska Street. . . . Forty SS soldiers and other soldiers in uniforms without SS insignia surrounded the group. Somewhere in the vicinity there stood a machine gun. I cannot describe the exact place, for I was too much upset at the time. . . .

"After the first salvo, wounded began to be visible in the crowd. The Germans then threw hand grenades. I saw a child emerge from the wounded belly of a pregnant woman. . . . I found myself next to the wall of the lavatories together with my children. My little son was seriously wounded in the back of the head. A grenade had wounded my daughter in the legs, belly, and chest. When everybody in the group had fallen, the Germans began shooting at any wounded who raised themselves or moved. . . . At twilight I managed to crawl into the lavatories together with my son and daughter, as well as sixteen-year-old Jadwiga Perkowska. My little son still showed feeble signs of life. . . ."[6]

Waclawa Szlacheta tells how a German detachment broke into her house and ordered about five hundred inhabitants out into the street. "I left the flat together with my husband, Mihal, born in 1895, my sons, Jozef, born in 1921 and Marian born in 1923, and two daughters, Lucyna, born in 1926 and Alina born in 1928. The gendarmes told us to halt at Sowinski Park. Men were separated from the women; boys older than about fourteen years of age were separated from their mothers. We were lined up against the fence of Sowinski Park from the gate of the park . . . up to the place where the stone cross stands. Women with small children stood at the gate up to the seventh pole of the fence. . . . Next stood the boys with the men."

She describes the positions of three machine guns from which "the German soldiers directed a salvo at us. I could not identify the formations of soldiers who were shooting at us. I am unable to say what uniforms they wore. But I heard voices speaking in German. I fell onto the ground at the second pole. . . . I was not wounded. Corpses were falling upon my legs. My youngest daughter, Alina, who was lying next to me, was still alive. I saw a soldier walk up to the perambulator containing the seven-month-old twins of my neighbor Jabuczyk, and

---

[6] Archives of the Central Commission for the Investigation of Nazi Crimes in Poland. 1100/Z/V K. 1056.

shoot them. . . . I am unable to state the exact time a German finished off my daughter, Alina. . . ."[7]

A year afterward, Willy Fiedler, a German prisoner of the Russians, talks of having seen several hundred Poles murdered in a tannery in Okopowa Street. "Until the moment they passed through the lateral building these poor people had no idea what was awaiting them. But the moment they entered the place where the corpses were piled up they became aware of the fact that they were about to be executed. The execution was performed by the same SS men who had escorted the Poles from the area behind the barbed wire. . . .

"Three of them watched the Poles in the courtyard, one bringing them in by groups . . . to the place with the corpses. A fourth SS man stood there on top of the corpses, shooting the Poles who were being forced to pile up there. The fifth SS man was dragging people to the piles. . . . I said to Captain Kleber that I was ashamed to wear a German uniform, to which the Captain answered that he did not understand who was issuing the orders to carry out these murders. . . . I do not know the names of any of the SS men. But they belonged to the combat group. I learned this from one of the SS men who told me."[8]

One could go on, but the affidavits are literally too many to be listed here. The gist of the Polish complaint is twofold. At the most, perhaps 50,000 men and women

[7] *Op. cit.* 1100 Z/V K. 1981.
[8] *Op. cit.* File B.D. 1402.

took part in the uprising. But according to both German and Polish sources, a total of some 250,000 died, and of these, about 30,000 were cremated in those first few days by *Verbrennungskommandos* in the area under Reinefarth's command.

In 1958, the author Tadeusz Klimaszewski came upon a German film producer who was looking for evidence with which to have Reinefarth indicted, and this meeting and the subsequent conversations brought back memories he had perhaps quite unconsciously been trying to suppress. The result was his book, *Verbrennungskommando Warschau*, and it is one of the most vivid, most terrible and particularized documentaries of the time.

*Der Spiegel* and the *Frankfurter Allgemeine Zeitung* have often in the past few years noticed Reinefarth's seemingly charmed life.[9] And that is what makes the Poles furious today, that Heinz Reinefarth has got away scot-free.

The American prosecutor at Nuremberg dismissed the charges against him "in view of the established absence of guilt." In 1949 the Poles asked the British forces in Germany to extradite him for trial. The request was refused "for security reasons."

[9] Both publications have commented on the case on several occasions. See, for example, the *Frankfurter Allgemeine Zeitung* for August 18, September 28, and October 9, 1958. On December 18, 1958, they even published an article, according to which Reinefarth claimed to have been in the anti-Nazi resistance. *Der Spiegel* of September 20, 1961, states categorically that radio announcements of August 5, 1944, prove beyond question that Reinefarth was in command in Wola.

In 1958 he was again cleared—by a German court this time, and in 1967 he was for the fourth time acquitted (once more by a German court). By this time he decided that he had never belonged "professionally" to the SS (although he had joined the organization on December 16, 1932, thus before Hitler came to power) and had, as a matter of fact, risked his life fighting the Nazi system whenever he could.

But the Polish case against him seemed so strong (after all, they, too, are perfectly reasonable people) that in the autumn of 1967 when I returned from Warsaw to London, I telephoned the Press Officer at the German Embassy to ask if he could tell me in his professional capacity just what the reasons for the latest acquittal had been.

To my astonishment, I had no sooner framed my question than the man shouted at me, "I have no time to listen to you."

"I am asking you in your capacity as Press Attache," I told him. "Is that the only answer you can give me?"

"Didn't you hear what I said? I have no time," he repeated.

Thus I would have had nothing except the Polish account to go on unless I had later discovered that Reinefarth claims that certain Polish documents are forgeries. But why should they bother, one asks oneself. Several thousand people were murdered. Someone was in command. Why pick on one man if he was innocent and another man was in fact guilty? Second, he claims he was not there at the operative time. Then the Polish documents to prove that he was must also be forgeries. Third, he says that there is no evidence to prove he ever gave any order for the murder of civilians. It is probably true that no *written* evidence still exists, or indeed ever existed. But if he gave no such order, it must have been given by someone under his command, and the general insists that it was done without his knowledge. Fourth, no witness has ever testified to having seen him present during an execution. In fact, no living German seems ever to have been present anywhere where anything evil was being done.

I would not think these happenings pertinent to a study of modern Poland, except that when we come later to consider Polish policy, both vis-à-vis the West and vis-à-vis its Socialist neighbors, we will see how such events—still not even acknowledged by the German establishment (only by the younger generation)—make any German-Polish rapprochement not only difficult, but impossible. They do more. They defeat Germany's own ends and strengthen bonds between members of the Eastern bloc which, without the memory of German horrors, horrors condoned by far too many Germans who want to have done with being blamed, might already be a fair part of the way down the road to dissolution.

It is no coincidence that Poland, which suffered the most, should cling more obstinately than any of its neighbors—not only to a Soviet alliance (that is under-standable), but also to Russian policies and patterns of thought that have nothing to do either with Socialism or her own real needs.

# 6. The Death of a City

COLONEL ZBIGNIEW ZALUSKI is a serious, tough but soft-spoken man in his late forties or early fifties. In June and July 1944 he came westward across the Bug River out of the Soviet Union, attached to the light artillery, First Polish Army. As soon as they had reached Polish soil, swarms of men turned up, anxious to join them, and these were sent back behind the lines for training. On the night of the thirtieth of July (he had fallen behind and then caught up with his regiment again near Jaworow), he was entrenched some sixty kilometers southeast of Warsaw.

The First and Second Polish Divisions were trying to get across the Vistula near Deblin (a drab little town near Pulawy). Zaluski's (the Third) was being held in reserve, and for several days he had nothing to do except wait impatiently for news from the front. Then they heard that the attempt had failed.

At Wilga nearer Warsaw the Russians did manage to send a few companies across, but no tanks and no heavy artillery. There they held a shallow bridgehead facing the Nineteenth Panzer, the Forty-fifth German Grenadiers, and the Hermann Göring Division.

But according to Zaluski, any effort at this time would have been useless, for the Red Army had overreached itself. The Russian summer offensive had begun on the tenth of June, and in some six weeks had advanced about four hundred miles to the Vistula. Now it was necessary to halt, reequip, and regroup.

It was roughly the tenth of August before Zaluski and his men actually heard about the uprising. Since they were obviously getting news from other fronts, this would indicate that the news from Warsaw was being deliberately withheld. By the fifteenth, censorship would have been useless anyway, for they were near enough to see the smoke of the burning city far off on the horizon. By this time a Russian tank regiment held a semicircular line just east of Praga and had begun bringing up heavy artillery.

Every night, south of the city there were probing attacks on the German positions. On the thirty-first of August three companies crossed the river again, and on the first of September there was an all-day battle against very strong German forces who were trying to keep their Ninth Army from being outflanked to the south. On the tenth the Russians attacked the suburb of Praga, lost 54 per cent of the assault force in killed and wounded, but after five days finally captured a large area just across the Vistula from Czerniakow.

Meanwhile, Polish units were moving north in an attempt (according to Zaluski) to cross the river at or near Warsaw and relieve their badly battered compatriots on the other side. They reached the railway bridge and could actually see the burning city and hear the rattle of machine gun fire. At night the western sky was punctuated with the fitful glow of little fires. On the sixteenth, under cover of darkness an officer by the name of Komornicki dived in and swam quite alone to the left bank, trying to establish some sort of liaison with the insurgents. At Saska two whole companies—four hundred men—got across, but the Germans had already pushed the rebels back from the river by this time, and were dug in on the western bank.

One small victory was the rescue of "Radoslaw," the heroic Colonel Janusz Mazurkiewicz who, after fighting for fifty days had had to be carried away wounded in a blanket tied to a couple of walking sticks because they had no stretchers. But by the middle of September the First Polish Army had lost 4000 men. Five battalions did manage to cross the river in the end, but according to Zaluski, not many men came back alive. Some forty-eight landing craft had been brought up by that time. Every single one of them was lost.

During the second half of the month there were fierce battles opposite Zoliborz to the north and Czerniakow to the south of the city. Three hundred and thirty guns were deployed per kilometer, and this surpassed by half as much again what the Russians had managed to throw in at Stalingrad.

And yet they had not been able to drive the Germans out of Warsaw. It had originally been the Russian plan to move forward well to the south and well to the north of the city proper, and this in fact is what was eventually done. Warsaw did not fall until the seventeenth of January 1945. By that time it was a dead city, of course, with not one single Pole—or even a German—left to guard the ruins.

Zaluski insists with quiet assurance that to have entered it in August or September would have been utterly impossible. "We are Poles," he said to me. "Can you really imagine that we did not try? I can assure you that ever since those days my troops have dreaded water."[1]

One of the most moving stories of the insurrection comes from Colonel Netzer of the AK, the Home Army, who fought in the far south of the city, in Czerniakow. According to him, until the twenty-fifth of August, his own sector remained relatively quiet. There were small-scale attacks every day, of course, but no major battle, for the Germans had decided to blot out the revolt district by district, and it was not yet Czerniakow's turn.

Down there they made themselves comfortable, organized supplies of food, blankets, beds, strung wires,

[1] All the preceding is from an interview with Colonel Zaluski in Warsaw on July 13, 1967. Colonel Zaluski was an officer of the First Polish Army, formed under Russian auspices in the Soviet Union.

and set up field telephones. They even found a printer among them and put out a daily newspaper of their own, *Czerniakow Walczy*. Every night Netzer himself slipped up to the city center past Jerozolimskie to find out what was happening. All too soon the pattern began to become clear.

On the eighth of August the Germans completed the capture of Wola. They were anxious to drive a wedge straight through the city from west to east. This would serve two purposes. It would ensure their lines of communication with their armies across the river and—equally important—it would cut Warsaw (and therefore the insurgent forces) in half.

On the eighth, Wola fell; shortly afterward, most of Powisle, and they had achieved their purpose. From then on, Zoliborz had to communicate with headquarters in Trzech Krzyzy by way of London. On the thirtieth of the month Warsaw's beloved old city, the Stare Miasto, fell after one of the cruelest battles of them all. Ten days later the Radoslaw group which had held out there against almost impossible odds crawled through the sewers (those that were left of them) to join their comrades holding out in Czerniakow.[2]

After the fifteenth of September there was no longer very much communication with anyone, and except for the forces commanded by Netzer and the rump of the

[2] And this journey was of course the subject of one of the finest of all postwar Polish films, Andrzej Wajda's *Kanal*, from the story by Jerzy Stefan Stawinski.

"Radoslaw" forces, the only insurgents still holding out were a pocket in the city center and those fighting in Zoliborz up to the north.

The German attack on Czerniakow came from Mokotow, just to the west. By the eleventh of September, having withstood daily assaults by Stuka dive-bombers, tanks, massed artillery, and even patrol boats on the river, both their battalion leaders and all their commanders had been killed. On the twelfth Colonel Netzer himself was wounded twice in the left wrist while firing from a window. They helped him down to the first aid post in the cellar, put his arm in a splint, and two hours later he was back on the firing line.

But shortly after that he was wounded again, and this time far too seriously to go on. His arm, his leg, and his left hip were smashed, so they carried him down a flight of broken stairs, laid him on a mattress, and from then on all he could do was appoint new officers to replace men as they died.

Of 1100 partisans under his command, almost half had already been killed. Of thirty-seven officers, only five managed to survive the war. Then on the night of the fifteenth the first Polish troops (the four hundred to whom Zaluski had alluded) came across the river to join them. This was a mistake, Netzer thought later, and Netzer, remember, was a Home Army man, not a Marxist. For, encouraged by their initial success, on the following two nights far larger numbers tried to get across (Zaluski's five battalions). But this time the Germans met them with a positively murderous fire and the casualties were enormous.

By the eighteenth (and Netzer still lying on his pallet) the area they held had been squeezed down to two streets, and on the following night it was decided to try to get the wounded (Netzer and about thirty others) off across the river in a dinghy fitted with pontoons. So they set out in pitch blackness, drifted downstream with six or seven men paddling, and just as they hit a pier of the Poniatowski Bridge opposite the middle of town, the span above them collapsed and Netzer was wounded for the third time.

At least the dinghy held firm against the bridge, but it was holed (so were the pontoons) and sinking, and now only five men and three women of the group were still alive. They managed to wrap Netzer in a blanket, and this took some time, for they had to freeze motionless every time a Very light went up from the German shore. As for the Colonel, he found it impossible to move, so he lay there, as much a philosopher as possible in the circumstances, with water up to his neck, the dead washing against him, listening to the firing and trying to gauge how accurate it was likely to become.

When at last it died down for a moment, his companions managed to pull him up onto the broken balustrade of the bridge. There he hung, head and shoulders in the roadway, feet in midair, and finally lost consciousness.

At dawn he awoke, very weak now from loss of blood, but none of them dared move, for of course they were clearly visible from the German trenches.

For four days and three nights they stayed in that position. On the third night the Russians in Praga at last laid down a smoke screen over the river, but the Germans, fearing an attack, began firing even more heavily into the dark. A shell landed on the bridge no more than two or three meters overhead. It smashed the Colonel's good leg and killed two of the remaining wounded who were lying beside him.

Then, toward dawn, he saw people coming out across the broken bridge from the Warsaw side, but in the poor light it was quite impossible to make out who they were. Nevertheless he called to them, and they came crawling toward him, pistols in their hands. They were five Polish fighters who had been hidden in a cellar. But no sooner had they reached him than the Germans saw them too, fired and knocked two of them off into the river.

By this time a lesser man might have begun to be discouraged, but when daybreak came the Colonel decided there was no point in lying there to die, so he tried to crawl off on his back, using his one good arm to pull himself along. But then suddenly two men and a girl appeared out of nowhere. He does not know to this day how they reached him, but they were Russians and they dragged him back through the water in his blanket over to the Russian side.

"When they got me to a field hospital," he says proudly, "they discovered I had eighteen wounds."[3]

But the uprising was not over yet. On the eighteenth the "Radoslaw" group had gone westward to Mokotow through the sewers.[4] Others were still holding out in Zoliborz. And in the city center Captain Zagorski and his men, as he recounts in *Seventy Days*, were actually being supplied with Russian arms.

And here we come to one of the most curious contradictions in the whole sequence of events. Zagorski recounts how on the fourteenth of September a Soviet reconnaissance plane had dropped a heavy sack onto their sector. It was found to contain black bread. On Monday, the eighteenth, however, their sentry at the gate reported other aircraft approaching, and this time they carried a far more valuable cargo.

It was well over a hundred Allied Liberator bombers, and they dropped cannisters. Some fell close enough to be retrieved. Men ran out to them and opened them feverishly, dragged out Sten guns and ammunition, tins of corned beef, antitank weapons, chocolate, revolvers. Cut off from the whole rest of the world, out of touch,

[3] This from an interview with Colonel Netzer in Warsaw on July 14, 1967. It ought to be pointed out that unlike Colonel Zaluski, whose account naturally reflected the Russian point of view, Colonel Netzer was an officer in the Armia Krajowa which took its orders from the exiled government in London.

[4] This writer lived for some weeks in the ulica Narbutta in Mokotow, now of course entirely rebuilt. To most of us in the West these Polish names are simply strange and difficult to pronounce. But to one who knows Warsaw and what took place there, they are almost awesomely evocative.

out of reach (as they had thought) of any friend, with only exhaustion, dust, wounds, and death around them, there in the cannisters they found the most moving gift of all—phials of blood for transfusions which bore labels in Polish and had been sent as a gift from the Polish hospital in Edinburgh.

Meanwhile Red Army planes were dropping weapons over other parts of the city. In a word, late in September, both the British and the Russians were sending in supplies. Yet the Russians would still not allow western aircraft to use the bases behind their lines. Now there was plenty of ammunition, but it had come too late. There was no longer any hope. Too many underground battalions had already been wiped out.

Zagorski tells what the last days were like, for him at least. His men, all those with whom he came in contact, were eager to fight on. But the Polish High Command, no longer seeing any prospect of relief, decided to surrender. Negotiations to this end lasted several days. It was agreed that the partisans should be treated as prisoners of war. No man would be punished for activities of any sort against the Germans during the occupation. And prisoners would be dealt with by the Wehrmacht, not by the SS.

So on Thursday, the fifth of October, they marched out at last from behind their barricades, those who were still alive, marched out carrying their rifles. And in spite of the fact that they had had no drilling, no manuals of arms, they marched well and not at all like beaten men between the long lines of Germans (many with cameras) who watched them come. Nobody would have guessed from their bearing that at least half of them were either sick or wounded.

Brown smoke was rising from out of the ruins on every side. Far off across the Vistula they could hear the desultory thunder of artillery. In Wola (for the Germans were marching them westward) they passed thousands of small white crosses that covered the Nazis who had died in the nine weeks' war.

No soldiers in any city in Europe had done what these Polish irregulars had done. In Warsaw, at least, east and west, Catholic and Jew, Communist and capitalist had fought side by side. There were even French and British prisoners who had come up out of hiding to join them. Between them they had held out for sixty-six days against what was still thought of as the finest army in the world.

According to Zagorski, they went into captivity as agreed, and in the main the Germans kept their promise. Most of those who surrendered survived the war. But it was many months afterward before they found out what had happened to Warsaw after they left it.

Hitler had ordered it leveled to the ground, and that is very nearly what the German army did. All civilians left alive were marched westward out of the city, either to camps in Poland or to forced labor in Germany itself. Then with the methodical industry of termites, Germans began ranging through the deserted buildings, seizing anything that could conceivably be said to have a value. Furniture, clothing, mattresses, blankets, heating appliances, electric cable, old iron, caches of food, all were moved out by the *Räumungskommando*. They are said to have filled 1500 railway wagons with packed suitcases alone.

Then, street by street as the houses were cleared, other troops went through with flamethrowers and set the buildings on fire. How many weeks it took to dynamite and burn down Warsaw no one was able to tell me, for there is not a Pole living who was there. But long before Christmas the job was done. Houses that still had a wall or two standing were planted with mines. And when the Germans were finished they simply cleared out to the west. Warsaw was never liberated. When the Red Army was ready to advance again it simply moved forward into the vacuum the Germans had left.

Poles who came back to the city in January 1945 say that the most terrible thing was to walk down the well-beloved streets, piled sometimes shoulder high with rubble, and to see the familiar facades of all the many houses. So that at first one felt that perhaps the damage was not so bad after all.

But then one realized that there was nothing except a cold January daylight shining behind the empty window frames. Yes, the facades were there. But nowhere was there anything beyond them.

It was Colonel Iwanczyk, "Stary Jakub," who provided what might be called the coda or postscript to this whole account.[5] He is a soldier of the old school, tough, uncompromising, a veteran Marxist, and a very serious student of military affairs.

He answered my questions thoughtfully, and told me the story of "his" war. Not only that. He told me how he and his companions had talked night after night in the woods near Kielce about the kind of Poland they wanted after the war.

"Gradually," he says, "I turned left in search of a program."

Of course we talked about the uprising in Warsaw, and he reflected the Party line reasonably accurately when he called it premature and said it had been organized from London purely for political reasons. (There is of course much truth in this.) They had unquestionably been brave men and women, he said. Even if they had turned out to be on opposite sides, politically, he felt a particular affection for that old warhorse, Netzer, with his eighteen wounds.

We ranged over the whole subject, he in a reminiscent mood about Kielce and the many comrades he, himself, had buried. Once he had been picked up by the Germans while visiting his own village. He and a dozen others had been ordered out to help comb the woods where they were hunting "bandits."

"I asked the Germans whom they were looking for,"

[5] In an interview in Warsaw, July 14, 1967.

he said, and for the first time a smile came over his face. "They were looking for me."

At the end of our talk we came back again to the subject of Warsaw. "Colonel," I said, "I've been told over and over again that there was nothing the Red Army could have done. Now, not as a Marxist, but purely as a military man, what is your opinion? Could the Red Army have relieved Warsaw at the time of the uprising?"

There was a long silence. I thought of those 330 guns per kilometer, and remembered the phrase, "Ever since those days my men have dreaded water."

Iwanczyk stared at me across the table until I decided that he did not actually intend to answer. But then unexpectedly he nodded.

"Yes," he said, and nodded several times more in confirmation. "Yes, they could."[6]

[6] Col. Iwanczyk, my interpreter, Mrs. Broniarek, and I had a coffee together at the end of this interview, and then the Colonel very obligingly drove us to the Journalist' Club where Mrs. Broniarek and I had another appointment. He and I parted in the friendliest possible manner, and certainly without haste.

In March 1968, I showed this section of the book to certain government representatives in Warsaw. They were horrified that the Colonel should have said anything that reflected on the good faith of their Russian allies, and called in Mrs. Broniarek to confirm the truth of what I had reported. This, of course, she did.

A month afterward, back in London, I received the following letter, which I am copying here verbatim.

Warsaw,
18 April, 1968.
Dear Sir,

I have learned from Interpress that my interview given at the Central Council office of ZBoWiD here in Warsaw was found quite interesting. Nevertheless, its last part calls for a supplement.

## The Death of a City

Whether or not this is true I do not know. Nor, I suspect, does anyone else. One question I did not ask. It would have been too discourteous an attack on a brave soldier. And that was—how could he explain the actions of the Red Army commanders at Wilno and Wolyn? In each of those places an entire division of AK partisan troops had welcomed the Russians as liberators. The Polish commanders had been invited to the Russian mess for a celebration dinner. There they had been arrested,

---

You asked me the following question: "In your opinion as a military man, could the Red Army have helped the Warsaw uprising?"

After thinking for a while, I replied, "Yes."

At that moment you thanked me and suddenly finished the interview. I did not have time to expand on this matter, although I wanted to add the following:

". . . and attempts *were* made to help. Due, however, to the enemy's military supremacy, these attempts could not really be of any importance. One of my colleagues, Col. Aleksander Klos, then *political* deputy commander of a battalion [italics mine. W.W.], has told me how his unit was crossing the Vistula, but the battalion could not get up onto the far embankment. For two days, soldiers hidden in the river willows were under a creeping German barrage. Out of 250 men only 29 returned alive to Praga. The others were killed. So far as I know, there were also other attempts to help the insurgents."

I intended to end our interview with this comment on the possibility Berling's troops had to help Warsaw and on the actual efforts that were made. If you find it acceptable, I am ready to support his statement.

I am afraid I cannot accept your version of our interview, ending with a simple, "Yes." I hope you will find it possible to add these few supplementary sentences. Otherwise I must ask you to leave out the last fragment of what you have written.

Sincerely yours,

Artur Wislicz-Iwanczyk

---

There the effect of political necessity on the truth as seen by a fine and honest officer. I leave it to the reader to judge (on the basis of this and other interviews) whether or not I have presented a fair picture of the facts.

and that same night their troops had been disarmed and the entire division shipped to Siberia.

By now, twenty-three years afterward, most of them have returned home.

# 7. The Rout
## of German Settlers—
## A Bleak Inheritance

IT was not until the seventh of May 1945, that the last German troops on Polish soil surrendered in Wroclaw. But months before that, German settlers (and indeed, indigenous Germans) had been fleeing westward in hundreds upon hundreds of thousands. It must have been a terrifying winter for those who had come east, looking for free land, as well as for those who had lived there generation after generation. From January when their offensive started until April, the Red Army kept driving across those endless plains, turning up out of the blue on every road, thundering into tiny hamlets, sometimes only hours after the evacuation.

It happened to be one of the worst winters in years. For weeks the temperature hovered between ten and fifteen degrees below zero, Fahrenheit. Yet well over a million Germans simply fled westward out of their villages in long columns, carrying whatever household goods they had been able to load onto their wagons.

The military had of course known for weeks that a Russian advance was inevitable. Yet there were no plans for an evacuation of civilians, and the hasty orders to flee westward, when they did come, came at the last moment when neither transport nor time was any longer available.

Motorized transport there was none, so the peasants used horses, and the horses, improperly shod, often fell on the icy roads, or floundered along for mile after mile, belly deep in snow. Those who lived in the cities had to travel by railway, mainly in unheated goods wagons or, if by road, in open, snow-covered trucks, but these often became stranded for lack of fuel. One saw people who had yoked themselves into sledges, carts, perambulators, even overturned tables loaded with their possessions.

One German officer writes about having witnessed "shattering scenes." Another describes the "awful sight of small children crushed to death in the crowds, or frozen to death, the mothers simply having to throw out their bodies because there was no time to get off the carts and bury them."[1]

Then there were frequent SS and even Wehrmacht patrols who pulled every man possibly fit for service off the trains and trucks, leaving the women and the aged to fend for themselves. By night the columns were attacked

---

[1] *Dokumentation der Vertreibung der Deutschen aus Ostmittel-europa.* Vol. I/1, p. 84. No date or place of publication given.

by German deserters and local Polish banditry bent on rape or plunder.

Mingling with all these terror-stricken multitudes were long columns of half-starved prisoners being driven west to prevent their liberation by the Russians, for of course there was no logic any more in anything. Sometimes these people would find the carcass of a horse by the roadside, break ranks and tear it apart with their bare hands, or with fists full of sharp stone.[2] Or in the midst of that crazy landscape, suddenly a long, straggling formation of Jews would appear, men who had somehow managed to survive the entire war, but now were being driven northward into the Baltic to be drowned. In other words, the enormous German clockwork mechanism had at last, and even by its own criteria, gone mad.

Trains and trucks, of course, would come under fire from Russian artillery or tanks. Wehrmacht and Red Army columns simply drove the refugees off the roads when they got in the way, pushed their vehicles into the ditches, and if they happened to need horses, took the horses.

Bridges were reserved for German troops, so civilians had to cross both the Vistula and the Oder by the occasional ferry or over the ice. It is ironic to reflect that these people—of Pomerania, Silesia, and Prussia, driven westward on orders from Berlin, were just those who, in

[2] *Op. cit.* I/1, p. 96.

the last free elections held in Germany, had given Hitler his handful of clear electoral majorities.

The evacuation of East Prussia, now cut off from the Reich by Russian forces, was an even more terrible affair. "Within several days almost all the population and very nearly all those who had been evacuated to the southern and western parts of East Prussia were drawn into a disaster which within a short period of time claimed the lives of at least 500,000 people."[3]

The pocket in the Vistula estuary was continually shrinking, and it contained hundreds of thousands of refugees who now tried to cross the twelve or thirteen miles of open water to the Vistula Spit that formed a barrier out against the open Baltic. All during January German ice breakers had kept a road of water clear, thirty meters wide across from the estuary. Wooden gangways had been set up alongside this road. But sometimes the wind-lifted water covered the ice as much as a foot deep, and people walking beside their carts had to wade through it.

Another German observer writes that "aged people sat or lay dying or frozen by the roadside along which the column moved, and no one paid the slightest attention to them. On the Spit itself, where the wave of refugees jammed up and masses gathered without a roof over their heads, conditions were unimaginable."[4]

Sometimes of course the ice would collapse under the

[3] J. Thorvald, *Es begann an der Weichsel*, Stuttgart, 1952.
[4] *Dokumentation*, I/1. p. 68.

weight of the laden carts. But nevertheless, those push-
ing along behind came thronging on in pell mell flight,
making a detour round the broken place, and all this
under almost continuous Russian air raids against the last
lines of communication of the German troops defending
Königsberg. It is a matter of some astonishment, not
only to this writer, but to the Poles as well, that any
German who survived that horror should ever want to
go back. As near as one can reckon, about half a million
succeeded in getting out—and about half a million died
in the attempt.

What Germans were left in what is now western
Poland were later evacuated by train—not in goods
wagons as the Germans allege, but in the same passenger
carriages that were used by the Allies to send Poles home
from the Reich. The Polish government took charge of
this forced migration, and by agreement with the occupying powers, sent part to the Russian, part to the
British zone in Germany. In the winter of 1946 there
were some deaths among these evacuees because the
trains were unheated, the lines were still in a state close
to chaos, and the journeys sometimes took far longer
than had been expected. When the authorities became
aware of these facts, evacuations were halted to await
warmer weather. In any case, by 1947, almost the last of
the Germans had been sent back into Germany. These
were followed in 1948–50 by a few prisoners and some
children who had lost their parents and been cared for in
Polish orphanages. After that date, with some very few

exceptions, there was not a German known to the authorities still left on Polish soil.

Now, at Yalta and Potsdam the victorious Allies had agreed among themselves that the Russians were to move their borders westward, roughly to the old Curzon line which constituted an inexact demographic frontier. Inexact, because although the countryside in the areas now acquired by the Russians was largely inhabited by Ukrainians, the old Polish cities of Lwow and Wilno were included.

Poland, by way of compensation, was to move westward too, taking Gdansk (formerly Danzig), half of what had used to be East Prussia, as well as the remainder of Silesia, Pomerania, and West Prussia. She was, in short, to wipe out the corridor that had caused so many difficulties, acquire a seacoast of some hundreds of kilometers and share a frontier with a much-reduced Germany on the Oder and Neisse rivers. This not only possessed the virtue of being a far more easily defensible border, it also gave Poland the rich Silesian industrial basin and a second great harbor in Szczecin (erstwhile Stettin) up in the northwest.

But even today, almost twenty-five years after the end of the war, Western Germany (indeed, Britain and America too) have not officially recognized this frontier. And yet it was Britain and the United States (in collaboration, of course, with the Soviet Union) who approved the change in frontiers in the first place.

Thus in November 1944, President Roosevelt wrote

to Stanislaw Mikolajczyk, head of the Polish government in exile: "In regard to the future frontiers of Poland, if mutual agreement on this subject, including the proposed compensation for Poland from Germany is reached between the Polish, Soviet and British governments, this government would offer no objection."

A month after that, on the fifteenth of December 1944, Churchill said in the Commons that "the Poles are free, so far as Russia and Great Britain are concerned, to extend their frontiers at the expense of Germany to the west."

At Potsdam, Great Britain, the United States, and the Soviet Union agreed that whereas the final delimitation of Poland's western frontier must await a peace settlement, Poland should thenceforward administer the territory which in fact she administers today. By "final delimitation," it seems reasonable to suppose, the powers meant only such mutually convenient minor adjustments as were made by the West German and Dutch governments after the war.

And yet even now, the official German position is that these Polish territories are still German. Germany, they say, has a right to her 1937 frontiers. If Hitler had won his war, Germany would have had no compunction about keeping what she had gained. Since he lost it, she can hardly expect to be treated as though she had never gambled in the first place.

There are signs, of course, that public opinion in Germany is gradually learning to accept the inevitable.

Even so, the Poles point out indignantly that all German maps (even the Shell Guides published in Germany) show these former German territories as German still. This even though there are no Germans left on present-day Polish soil, even though some eight million Poles have taken the place of the Germans who used to live there, even though Poland has built up a tremendous industrial complex in these former German territories, as well as whole cities such as Wroclaw, which are inhabited by a fresh, young, and enthusiastic generation of Poles who were born there.

As a matter of fact, Silesia split between Germany and Poland as it was before the war, did not even make economic sense. All in all, Poland acquired some 101,000 square kilometers of former German territory. This had constituted 21.4 per cent of Germany's total area, but had been inhabited by only 13.8 per cent of her population. Over a million Poles had lived there too. But in 1939, this area had accounted for only 5.9 per cent of German industrial output.

The reasons for this backwardness are not far to seek. Simply stated, these are the considerable distances of factories here from their markets in Germany, the predominance in the area of small industrial enterprises and large Junker estates, and the long-continuing emigration (the *Ostflucht*) of the more adventurous who looked for a richer life in the Rhineland.

In the production of steel, of electricity, of pig iron, even of agricultural products, these areas contributed far less per capita than did any other part of the country. In addition, the great coal and steel complex of Katowice was split right down the middle, and had therefore to be worked uneconomically.

As early as the nineteenth century, Bismarck had been concerned at how little the east contributed to her own support. In 1928 special funds had had to be set aside in Berlin for economic aid to East Prussia. Indeed, by 1931, specially reduced taxes and interest rates had been introduced for all the eastern territories. And these subsidies continued until the very outbreak of war, for eastern Germany had been valuable chiefly in the event of hostilities when its agricultural surplus could be used to help feed the rest of the country.

Today what are now the western territories of Poland have a far different look about them. And partly for these reasons, partly because of the Poles' hideous memories of the occupation, partly because they have made these into *de facto* Polish territories, there can never be any question of negotiation about them. Responsible German politicians are perfectly aware of the fact. Willy Brandt has more or less said so in public. But until it becomes the settled policy of the Bonn government, there can be no hope whatever even of starting talks that might lead to the reunification they profess so ardently to desire.

In any case, this shift of the nation westward and the consequent flight or deportation of the Germans was followed by a migration of Poles, themselves, of almost incredible proportions. Huge numbers of people from the poverty-ridden areas of the southeast which had become part of the Soviet Union moved as far as they were able up to the northwest in the neighborhood of Szczecin. The city of Lwow moved almost *en masse* to Wroclaw. In both cases the moves were made for obvious reasons, to escape Russian domination and to go to a part of the country where land and houses were to be had for the asking.

One man, a ship's captain, described his own family's move to what used to be East Prussia. "My father had been killed," he said. "I was only fourteen, but I thought of myself as the head of the family. And even then I loved the sea. So I got out a map, stuck my finger on a village up near the coast, and said to my mother and little brother, 'That's where we're going. There!' So we did, got a travel voucher, arrived, moved into the first decent, empty house we could find, and that was that."

In the first years, Polish sociology had a field day, studying the mixture of populations in the new towns. As the Mayor of Wroclaw, Dr. Iwaszkiewicz, said to this writer, "One used to be able to distinguish the various grains in the porridge. But by now there's been so much intermarriage and so many hundreds of thousands have been born here that we'd never be able to disentangle them again." And it is strange indeed to see how different sorts of society grew up, depending upon where people went. Today the citizen of Szczecin and the citizen of Olsztyn are utterly unlike one another, and torpid Poznan is a different kettle of fish indeed from bubbling Wroclaw. But more of these things anon.

In a word, during the very first months after the end of the war the last of the Germans were flung out and the Poles were once more masters in their own house. And that was all very well and proper, except that almost the whole of the nation lay in ruins. Twice in a generation the German and Russian war machines had rumbled across Poland and rumbled back again. Early in 1945 the Russian armies executed a rapid pincer movement round Cracow and forced the German troops there to flee before they had time to destroy the city. More or less the same thing happened in Gdynia, where only the harbor installations were destroyed. But these are the only instances I have been able to find of any army making an effort to save Polish property.

Mostly it was not so. In the winter and early spring of 1945 the Socialist government that had been formed in Lublin came in with the Red Army, found itself rooms and offices as best it could in Warsaw, and set about trying to survey the devastation.

There had been talk of setting up a temporary capital in Lodz, which had been comparatively little damaged. But one thing the Poles wanted above everything else was a sense of identity and continuity. A provisional capital, no matter how convenient, would constitute a break with the past. The last Polish kings, the last free Poles had governed from Warsaw, and

Warsaw might be dust, ashes, felled trees, and broken roads, but it was back to Warsaw they were going.

That decision having been made, there could be no special consideration for government officials. They simply had to make do like everyone else. So the first Minister of Finance slept on top of his desk with a briefcase for pillow. His assistant set up a typewriter on a wooden crate and used the typewriter case for a stool. At night he opened an umbrella over his bed because although he had a ceiling, he had no roof. And when, very early on, he was ordered to Sweden to see what he could do about selling coal, he protested that the honor of Poland required him to wear both a necktie and a pair of untorn shoes—and he possessed neither.

One finds it difficult today to imagine a civilized European nation that owns no foreign exchange whatsoever, no railways, no factories or power plants, no dams or dikes or reservoirs, whose few available trucks belong to the military, whose very roads have been torn up and pitted with shell holes, whose harbors are filled with wrecks and rotting hulks that lie listing in the undredged channels.

The facts are overwhelming. According to figures submitted at the International Reparations Conferences in Paris in 1946, Poland's material losses had amounted to almost seventeen billion prewar dollars. Thirty-eight per cent of her total fixed assets had been destroyed. The damage was three and a half times as great as that she had suffered in World War I. Twenty-two per cent of her population had been killed and another 2½ per cent more or less permanently disabled. A second 25 per cent had either been locked up in prison, driven away to forced labor—or had simply fled to the forests. And of those that were left, the great majority were suffering from malnutrition.

The very farms and fields had become almost unworkable. The land, they say, is something you cannot take away. But about two fifths of the farm buildings had either been set on fire or blown up, and several millions of acres had been mined. Not only that. About half the country lay fallow because peasants had simply fled, so the production of food had declined catastrophically. Some areas only had 4 per cent of their prewar numbers of pigs and 8 per cent of the cattle. As for the railways, they were in a particularly fearful state. About 9000 kilometers of track had been torn up and 100 kilometers of bridges and viaducts. Of course rolling stock itself hardly existed.

One could go on listing the damage, but the point has surely been made. We must make our brief statement of devastation here, however, so that it will be clear where present-day Poland began and so that her achievements may be set in some sort of perspective.

In 1945 there were so many obvious priorities that it was difficult even to choose between them. As a matter of fact, the government chose transport. But it could have done nothing without the unpaid, voluntary assistance of vast numbers of the population. Those early days of peace must have been like a springtime after some interminable winter. In Wroclaw people dared not walk in the streets when it was windy for loose stones were constantly falling off the facades of houses. But on the first really warm summer day of 1946, fire engines were brought out to clean the streets, and suddenly in pure high spirits firemen began playng hoses on the watching crowds. Nobody was angry. People simply stood where they were and laughed, with water pouring down their faces. It is difficult for us to whom the war now seems remote to remember the spirit of cooperation, of camaraderie, of common effort, and a sense of common achievement.

It must have been then that Poles of every possible political persuasion acquired the habit of referring to *our* city, *our* factory. *We* are building a block of flats over there, they will say. So for month after month as they drifted back to the city and somehow found shelter, scores of thousands of Warsovians, men, women, the poor and the not so poor reported of their own free will to the gangs that were clearing up rubble. Today it seems almost inconceivable that literally 75 per cent of the city had to be hauled away by horses and carts before they could even start to rebuild. Weekends, holidays, during the long summer evenings, one would see people passing buckets and trundling wheelbarrows, digging away with picks and shovels. Sometimes they would find a wall still bloody or with remnants of matted hair on the brick.

People came drifting back too from prisoner of war or forced labor camps, looking for relatives, searching through the ruins for messages nailed to the walls.

"Wladek, we have gone to Aunt Anna's in Konstancin."
Or one would see a sign reading, "No mines."

One informant who spent twelve hours a day hunting
export markets (there was of course a desperate need for
foreign currency) told how for the first year and a half
he had to work by candlelight. Finding sheets of glass
for windowpanes was a problem too. What generally
happened was that you finally ran down a bit, but it
turned out to be the wrong shape or size. So you simply
bricked in your window space to fit the piece you had—
and then found you couldn't read because not enough
light got in.

Water came from the well, of course, and when it
came your turn to fetch coal at the depot (naturally
there were no deliveries) you asked for the day off and
borrowed a hand cart. You knew perfectly well you
were going to have to queue for five or six hours.

Anyway, in 1945 the group of Communist-trained
Polish politicians and economic planners came in on the
shoulders of the Red Army and set about building a
bankrupt wilderness into a modern state. As in most of
Eastern Europe, they inherited a peasant economy and
decided to turn it into an industrial one.

But they started under a worse handicap than the
planners did anywhere else. Even in 1939, Poland had
lagged far behind her neighbors. As far as the industrialized western nations were concerned, she might as well
have been in the nineteenth century.

And the reasons for this go back a very long way
indeed. Four hundred years ago Poland was a nation of

petty landowners, the *szlachta*, or minor nobility. A *szlachcic* might be the landlord of a muddy hamlet. He might, on the other hand, own as little as three or four acres which he tilled himself.

And for all practical purposes, this *szlachta*, ignorant and impoverished though it may often have been, ruled the nation. For the monarch was never able to act without its approval, and that approval (since the gentry was proud, individualistic, and ill-educated) often took an interminable time to acquire.

In other parts of Europe stronger ruling houses brought about a certain centralization of power. In other parts of Europe towns grew up to balance this sort of primitive squirearchy. But towns depend upon industry, and Polish property, when an owner died, was by immemorial custom divided and subdivided among his heirs. So no one (or very few) ever acquired the capital without which industry cannot come into existence.

Therefore no industry ever came into being. Manufactured goods were generally imported—and expensive. Agricultural produce was cheap. This kept the peasant poor. Indeed, they say that within living memory a peasant would normally split a match in two before he lighted half of it.

But this was only a part of Poland's handicap. Being decentralized, she had always been a natural prey to her more unified and therefore more powerful neighbors. Prussia, Russia, and Austria had all been ruled by strong monarchies. The conquest and partition of Poland were therefore inevitable, and when in the late eighteenth century this occurred, the state of the Polish economy, indeed, one might even say the development of the Polish character, were determined for the next two hundred years.

Western Europe grew into the industrialized nations we know today. Poland stayed on the farm, and since the soil was thin and the capital for development nonexistent, even the Polish farm fell behind the farm of its German or Danish neighbor. And of course what managerial posts there were went not to Poles (the law went so far as to prohibit it), but to the Russian, the Austrian, or the Prussian, depending on where in Poland one was.

Thus no managerial class was ever allowed to grow up in Poland. With some very rare exceptions, no Pole was ever trained in administration. No Pole ever learned twentieth-century industrial techniques, whether in the board room or on the factory floor. Not even the railways and post office were Polish, and so little impact was the Pole allowed to have on his own country that even today one can detect a very clear difference in architecture, in landscaping, in the very character of the people in the three separate parts into which the country had been divided.

Under partition, Poles learned to be dilatory, unpunctual, unworkmanlike, and irresponsible, for it never paid them to be anything else. Indeed, to feign ignorance often kept one out of trouble. In the long run it led to real ignorance too, but that was a different matter.

The only thing that did not die during all those dark centuries of battle and enslavement was a burning patriotism, a terrible and wonderful urge to keep not only the idea of a nation, but the very language of the nation alive. There were times, of course, when even to speak Polish was against the law. There was a time in Poznan when a man was not allowed to marry unless he could produce evidence of an ability to speak and understand German. It was all to no avail. Poland as an idea and Polish as a language survived. If the peasants did nothing else, this one thing they did.

Then came the terrible first world war and a devastation like nowhere else in Europe, but as a result of it, in 1918 the nation was at last reborn. Yet even then she did not come into her own. For twenty years she was ruled by a succession of ambitious, brave, and reasonably honest mediocrities, army men with no experience of government. The two exceptions were an officer with a burning hatred of Russia. That was Pilsudski. And a gentleman with a burning love for music. That was Paderewski. Neither was fit to lead a nation up out of the Middle Ages.

After that—1939, with what result we know, and then 1945 with a new breed of men in power, men who for all their intelligence had no more experience than their predecessors in the details of practical government. Still nowhere the desperately needed managerial or industrial training.

That was how it started. That was the inheritance, and it is with these facts in mind that we must now look at what has failed in the experiment and what has been achieved.

# 8. The Face of Poland

BEFORE they could make a start they had to repair at least some of the damage, and the prospect must have been enough to make one despair. It was hard to believe such carnage would ever be set right or—if it could—to know where one ought possibly to begin.

But within a very short time the railways were more or less back in service and the harbors were cleared. By 1947 most farmland had been rid of mines, and in every city huge concrete blocks of flats had begun rising, tier on tier out of the ruins. Walls and ceilings, they will tell you, had to come before aesthetics (though I think they have carried this principle too far), so today there are no longer families without roofs of their own. Flats are small, jerry built, and noisy (people jumbled all of a heap on top of each other), but at least it is no longer impossible to find a place to live.

Now, all backward countries have one thing in common, a disproportion of labor to fixed capital assets, and in postwar Poland this was true with a vengeance. So the planners' first object was to create those missing fixed assets, and sometimes it must have looked as though it were going to have to be done out of thin air. In the beginning they could not even manufacture a power plant, and huge quantities of both raw materials and machinery had to be bought from abroad. Indeed, as one expert said to me (he was manager of a factory manufacturing nitrates), "I got back to Tarnow in 1946 and looked around. We couldn't even mix cement for the walls until we'd rebuilt the water system, and to do that we had to mix cement to make piping to carry the water."

Aside from the general devastation that had to be made good, their greatest need was to build a chemical and an engineering industry, for both are fundamental to any modern economy. And of course all initial installations for these too had to come from overseas. To pay for such purchases they had two assets and two assets only—sweat and coal. In the period 1949–55, coal made up 60 per cent of Polish exports.

As the Russians had done, as indeed orthodox Marxian economics is everywhere interpreted as demanding, they decided to build up heavy industry at the expense almost of every other need, for this in turn would make it possible for them to manufacture goods on their own. To do this, to create capital assets, they had to plow back a far greater proportion of income than would have been

usual in any normally prosperous society. The individ-
ualist, the entrepreneur, those used even to the mildest
forms of luxury in Western Europe would have been up
in arms at the thought of having to sacrifice personal
comfort in the interests of public good. But the Poles
had no luxuries to be used to. In those early days, the
priorities were so blatantly plain, the need for a central
authority with a plan—any plan—so self-evident, that
there was remarkably little opposition to what the government proposed.

In much of the west, and particularly in the United
States with its slogan, "Better dead than Red!" it is
difficult not only to be objective, but even to see with
other eyes than one's own. But we shall not understand
contemporary Poland unless we are able to look not
only at economics, but also at the postwar political situation through Polish eyes.

To put it in a nutshell, the Poles have discovered that
for whatever reason, be it character or geographical situation or what you please, they have rarely been able to
stand as a viable unit on their own. Germany as well as
Russia have been, are, and probably always will be immensely more powerful. Both of these neighbors, as is
only natural, are ruled almost entirely by self-interest.
Left alone, Poland was like a kitten between two fighting cats. Western alliances had got them nowhere. Na-
poleon acquired a Polish mistress but he did not end partition. England and France, to be sure, had gone to war
in 1939 on Poland's behalf, but one of these allies had

suffered a humiliating defeat and the other, for all the help she brought, might as well have been at the ends of the earth.

So the only possible ally for Poland is one or the other of her powerful neighbors. An alliance with Germany is unthinkable. An alliance with the Soviet Union has disadvantages too. We shall have something to say later about Poland's reasons for feeling both fear and contempt for the Russians. Few Poles profess any love for them. But at least Marxism is for better or worse an attempt to inject reason and justice into the still only half-understood science of economics.

But let us go a step further and look at the other side of the coin. To oppose a system—any system—one must have some feasible alternative to put in its place, and no Pole with memories of prewar days has any experience of either just or rational government. If the only alternative to the present praesidium is Colonel Beck or Marshal Rydz-Smigly, or even the clerical conservatism of, say, Portugal, the majority of Poles would probably vote for the praesidium. For that can eventually—as in Czechoslovakia—be made to marry a degree of liberal democracy to the virtues of Socialist planning. That a British or Scandinavian parliamentary system might be preferable to either of the present alternatives is beside the point. That alternative has simply never even been a possibility.

We have to visualize Poland too as the geographical unit into which—after all her permutations—she has developed. The program of industrialization, of agricultural development, the growth of the cities, the war between government and Church, the almost explosive diversity in modern Polish theater, painting, poetry, and cinema (because this, too, is a geographical diversity), none of these can be seen in any sort of perspective unless we can also see the physical facts, unless we know just what Poland looks like twenty-five years after the war.

Fundamentally it is one vast river system, the Vistula's, with highland watershed, the long, meandering stream and its many, many tributaries that all lead north to the wide, flat estuary up near Gdansk on the Baltic. A system and a half, one should say, for if the Vistula dominates southern, central, and eastern Poland, the Oder forms a large part of her boundary to the west. Most of her major cities are linked by water. Thus Torun, Bydgoszcz, Cracow, Warsaw itself are on the Vistula. Wroclaw and Szczecin are on the Oder, Poznan and Czestochowa on the Warta that flows into it.

Up in the northwest corner in Szczecin province, long, flat, alluvial fields, tumbledown farms, and peasants who are migrants, all of them (for this was German territory), migrants from the poverty-ridden villages between Rowno and Pinsk. It is unfair to the Poles to begin by describing Szczecin, for Szczecin is not only untypical; it is plagued with problems peculiar to itself. Only in the past generation have these Szczecin peasants been taught to read and wear shoes on weekdays. They are the drabbest specimens of humanity that I saw in all of Poland.

For (quite unwarrantably) this is one of the two poorest areas in the country (the other being down in Bieszczady in the southeast), and although they tell one that Szczecin is the busiest port in the Baltic, surpassing even Leningrad and Copenhagen, one's first impression is of damage unrepaired, narrow roads pitted with potholes, and on every side an almost unutterable desolation.

In the seventeenth century the Swedes seized Szczecin from the Poles, and in 1720 sold it to the Prussians, who held it until 1945. Perhaps its drabness can be explained by the fact that, unlike Wroclaw, it never had a strong Polish minority, unlike Poznan it has no industry worth mentioning, and unlike almost anywhere else in Poland, its population is not predominantly young.

Whatever the reason, the villages round about are ramshackle places too, with tins, broken bottles, and scraps of paper littering the untended gardens, with their few orchards gone to ruin, their very churches derelict, their peasants often still barefooted and almost invariably unshaved, with cottages that have holes in their roofs, scraggy hens fluttering in and out through their broken windows, with dirt and idleness visible wherever one looks.

I spent a whole day wandering from hamlet to hamlet along this frontier. Here a farmer who admitted with a shrug that he never got out into the fields until noon. There a young woman sitting in a doorway, gazing

lackadaisically at her feet. Normally she woke at nine
when the baby cried. What was the use of getting up
earlier? The more one did the more there was to do. In
the next farmyard, a grandmother in the nearest thing
possible to rags, her face and neck seamy with accumu-
lated filth. No, she would not like to go back to the
Soviet Union. The Ukrainians there had used to beat
them because they were Polish.

And this was the picture over and over again. Of
course it is dangerous to generalize. One wants a social
psychiatrist, not an economist to understand these people. For if they are poor (their soil is not at all bad), if
their crops looked uneven, their cattle lean, their habita-
tions (one ought not to call them houses) insufferably
vile, one can blame neither the climate, the war, nor the
government, only their own ignorance (they belong in
the seventeenth century), their long history of oppression as a minority, and the concomitant consumption of
vast quantities of vodka.

Up in the far north of this region there are a few tiny
fishing villages and one gem of a seaside hamlet (Nowe
Warpno) where the houses seem more tidy and the
drunks more recently washed. In Szczecin itself, they
show one newspapers printed by right-wing organiza-
tions in the Reich, describing how this village has gone
downhill under Polish occupation, how in that the
church roof has fallen in. One reads with very mixed
feelings, shrugs, listens to Polish plans for rebuilding, for
enlarging the port, for developing the shipyard. One

listens and then heads eastward along that windy, northern coast into the heart of Poland.

Gdansk and Gdynia are almost twin cities with the little resort of Sopot like a many-colored brooch between them. In summertime the bikini girls come swarming there from all over Poland (in February they migrate to Zakopane for the skiing), and the art exhibitions, the narrow streets and bright cafes, the boardwalk and the longest pier in Poland stretching out to sea, the great curve of the northward-looking beach and the very grand Grand Hotel itself probably have as many enchanting faces per acre as any other spot in the world.

By late afternoon the cafes are swarming with jeans, head scarves, ice-blue eyes, and lithe bodies that have hair like cornsilk flopping onto their shoulders. At night they are in the discotheque, listening to Bulgarian versions of the Beatles and the Rolling Stones. Or they are dancing. Or if the boy friend of the moment is flush, they are dining at the Grand where foreigners pay almost twenty dollars for a bottle of whiskey and half as much again for a good French brandy.

There is one enormously fat man with what seems to be a large income of which nobody knows the source. His name is Rzeszotarski, and he is known all over Poland for collecting pretty young women in his red Mustang convertible and driving them from party to party. I have heard him tell stories about them, the famous girls of Sopot, while he consumed eight eggs, half a dozen slices of toast, and four cups of coffee as a midmorning snack.

"They're an idle lot," he said. "The spoiled generation. Well, I like to spoil myself too, so I feed on them. And by the end of the season you can have any one of them for a promise of breakfast."

Mr. Rzeszotarski is a very rich man, a very gross and lonely man. One can only hope (perhaps wistfully) that he is mistaken.

Gdansk (which the Germans called Danzig) was a splendid medieval city almost entirely destroyed during the war. So with that passion they have for providing themselves with roots, the Poles have rebuilt it almost stone by stone as it was, the carvings, the balustrades and terraces, the palely colored housefronts, the wide streets white as marble. It never was a German city, they tell you, although at several periods in history its population was predominantly German. The name, Danzig, they say, was simply a Germanization of Gdansk, which came in turn from Gothic *guda* (modern Polish *woda*) meaning water.

Schopenhauer was born there, and Fahrenheit. So was the great astronomer, Hevelius. And today one of the most charming and learned gentlemen in Poland, Dr. Marian Pelczar, is the city librarian. He will sit by the hour and tell you the history of Gdansk with such enthusiasm and such weight of wisdom lightly borne that he can make any listener an enthusiast too.

One of his tales that struck a very living chord was of

a massacre of Poles in Gdansk by the Teutonic Knights in 1308. The only record we have is in the correspondence of the Pope, Clement V, who, writing to the head of the Order, states that he has had a complaint from the Poles and wishes to know the truth of the matter.

The reply from the Teutonic Knights is worthy of the sophistication of a modern politician. The phrase "credibility gap" comes to mind when we read that the Poles had several bandits living among them. Upon application from the Knights for the surrender of these bandits, the Poles in Gdansk responded with alacrity. They not only handed over the culprits. In horror at having (albeit innocently) sheltered them, they burned their own houses, killed a few of their wives, and went off into the hinterland, nobody knew where.

In spite of its artists, its students, its color, and its very great beauty (as though a medieval Hanseatic town had been re-created in front of our eyes), Gdansk struck me as being still more a museum than a place to live. It will take a century to re-weather it. But that is a matter of opinion. As in Gdynia, however, they have founded a new shipbuilding industry of which they are quite justifiably proud, for Poland has never been a maritime nation.

Go farther east into what used to be East Prussia, through Olsztyn and Gizycko, past the hundreds of Mazurian lakes that lie in the folds of the pine-covered hills. A morning mist rises over the blue-black water, and even in gentle rain the far slopes are invisible.

Narrow, white passenger boats slip between the locks and tie up below the big hotels. Busloads of factory workers and plump wives come chuddering along the narrow roads, and in the evenings they sit in the restaurants eating herring with sour cream, stuffed cabbage, bigos and salad, laughing, the men slowly getting drunk, the women bold and bawdy. On dark quays under the trees loudspeakers pour out their potpourri of news and culture, Mozart and exhortation. Nobody listens. The wind blows soft and clean off the lake. Men tinker with boats in the shallows. Gulls come drifting in from the Baltic and skim across the invisible surface of the water.

Up in Mazuria too, one comes upon the first of the state farms, hundreds, or it may be thousands of acres bought in from peasants who have either moved to the towns or simply retired. These are quite different from collectives. They are farms run by a manager who is a government employee, and who in turn employs farm labor which owns no share of the land. East Prussia was a country of large estates which the Poles took over as going concerns at the end of the war, so there are greater numbers of state farms here than in most other parts of the country. One sees tractors in the fields and combine harvesters, which individual peasants can rarely afford. Indeed, for reasons which will become apparent, the government has great plans for these combines.

South and east again. The hills flatten out and there lies Bialystok sprawling, made of wood with great concrete slabs of buildings interspersed among the old-fash-

ioned porches and gables that might have come out of
Gogol or Turgeniev—or Bielsk Podlaski with its wide
streets and the old, old wooden houses, brown as weath-
ered coffins with wooden shutters over the windows and
here and there an old flake of blue or rose-colored paint
to show you what color the house was back in the nineteenth century.

Here the soil is thin and the people are thin but the
one restaurant serves a memorable lunch. Go farther
still, east to the Russian border, and you come to something far more interesting, Bialowieza, which, except for
bits of Scandinavia, is the last primeval forest in all
Europe.

It is a ghostly place, for no cars are allowed there,
only the long, narrow Polish carts that lurch softly along
the forest paths. Here the oaks live six and eight hundred
years and fall, when they fall, to die and rot in the damp
undergrowth, for no one in Bialowieza is allowed to
disturb the course of nature. There is no pruning, no
felling, no gathering of brush or building fires. Mush-
rooms grow in the livid shade and no one picks them.
Bees live in high holes in the trees, and under their
entrances the rusted spikes some peasant put there eighty
or a hundred years ago to keep out his competitor, the
wild bear. The fox or the lynx slip through the brush,
and no one hunts them. There are wolves here, wildcats,
the largest herd of European bison in the world, and
ornithologists have counted two hundred and thirty
varieties of birds. Among them, one sees hawks circling

far overhead in an almost illimitable sky and the great Polish eagle that can drop like a stone out of the sun onto an unsuspecting hare.

Here the hunting lodge where the Tsars came with their retinues and the now silent glades where they rode. Here there is even an English park laid out, an eighteenth-century landscape between two lakes, with paths and follies, arched bridges, and perspectives of which Capability Brown would not have been ashamed. And only a mile or two away from the depths of the forest, the moon shines down at night on wide and shimmering lawns that might very well be in Surrey.

A little to the south and we have reached the middle of the country. In an irregular line from east to west, from Janow Podlaski on the Bug, stretch Warsaw, Lodz, and Poznan. This is the rich center of all Poland, the heartland.

Janow Podlaski itself is a 4000-acre stud farm that has just celebrated its hundred and fiftieth birthday. Here low, white buildings, neat barns and stables (built in the mid-nineteenth century), and in the fields about three hundred and fifty Arabs and half Arabs, the former sold largely to England and America, the latter to local peasants.

The manager, a tall, courteous man called Krysztalowicz, sits in the sunlight gazing out across an exercise yard and talks quietly about how when the Germans took his horses west he went with them in the cattle trucks, and how when it became possible to bring them back he brought them back to Janow Podlaski. He points out the neat little houses of the trainers, walks with you down across hot and sleepy meadows, telling a story about this animal and that, gesturing as he describes the set of shoulder and neck, the architecture of the head—talking horses, always horses. Fifty years ago they bred them long-legged for cavalry officers. Now they breed them more stockily for work.

With some pride he shows you his herd of Friesians, for they keep cattle too to help balance the budget. Women milk them three times a day, for in most of Poland milking is thought of as woman's work, degrading for a man. And as Krysztalowicz talks he strolls the hundred yards or so with you to the Bug that meanders idly northward between its clumps of alder and young willow. Across that narrow water is the Russian frontier, the border of Byzantium, and although you are assured that a Russian sentry is probably watching through binoculars, nowhere is there a single soul to be seen.

Almost due west of here is Warsaw, that veritable phoenix among cities, battered, God knows, with bullet marks still visible on many walls, but with whole districts rebuilt, and its old town, its Stare Miasto (like Gdansk) reconstructed almost in minuscule detail as it was before.

Farther west still, the big, sprawling industrial city of Lodz with its film studios, and westward farther yet, the rich farmlands of Wielkopolska and the city of Poznan.

But we shall come round to Warsaw and Poznan in their turn.

We were in the east, on a line between Janow Podlaski and Warsaw. Head south from there, and you come to Radom with its rather astonishing elegance and stately streets, to Kielce, capital of the province and the Swietokrzyskie hills where the witches hold their sabbath, where peasant women wear capes with red or green and black vertical stripes, and where so many of the partisans hid out during the war.

South and east, and you come upon what is to me the loveliest part of the country, the province of Lublin, with long, slightly rolling fields, with slow, willow-fringed rivers, and beautiful distances. It is a terribly neat and yet varied countryside. One thinks of Rupert Brooke . . .

> Great clouds along pacific skies,
> And men and women with straight eyes,
> Lithe children lovelier than a dream,
> A bosky wood, a slumbrous stream,
> And little kindly winds that creep
> Round twilight corners, half asleep.

Long before dawn old women are out with besoms, sweeping the village streets. At five or six o'clock of a summer morning whole families are riding their long carts to market. In winter the drifts pile up behind the hurdles along the roadside. By late afternoon the almost incredibly handsome, well-made children go past on their way home from school.

In almost every village, alongside the notices of taxes due and local regulations, one sees photographs of recent road accidents. As drivers the Poles are mighty individualists. One shudders to watch a man weave at forty miles an hour between strolling couples, horn going the whole time. Or—it must be an exception—I have seen a man in a hired car deliberately skim close to girls in white stockings and white summer dresses to make them leap back into a puddle. They overtake on blind curves. They race each other; they do the impossible to prove what brave and skillful drivers they are—and their accident rate is enormous. Drunken driving was so common that it has now become an indictable offense to drive with any alcohol whatsoever in the bloodstream. And the punishments for those who are caught are so severe that I have never seen a Polish driver willing to "have one for the road."

If you are found to have over 0.5 per cent of alcohol in your blood, you can lose your license for as much as ten years, and even if there has been no accident you can be imprisoned for two. I was told of one television producer who actually killed a girl passenger by driving drunk into a bollard on his way home from a party. The court gave him seven years.

Below Pulawy, Kazimierz on the Vistula, then Lublin on its little hill (Majdanek just a mile away), and farther southeast, Zamosc, built in the Italian renaissance style like Padua, with rich little farms on every side of it. Southeast again, and you have gone as far as you can go, to the fortress town of Przemysl at the base of the steep Carpathians that form the long, irregular frontier with Czechoslovakia.

So the whole of southern Poland is mountainous. If we turn west along the slopes of the hills past Rzeszow and Tarnow, we come almost at the source of the Vistula to Cracow, the finest city in Poland, the site of a Cardinal's palace, a fourteenth-century university, and of Wawel Castle, the seat of the Jagiellonian kings.

Wawel is like Hampden Court without the gardens, the same series of state rooms leading one out of the other, with walls of Spanish leather, with Breughels and Tintorettos in unexpected corners. Down in the crypt, the graves of a hundred Polish kings and queens—from little Jadwiga who died young (one is shown her window seat) and gave her gold to the university, to Jan Sobieski who saved Vienna from the Turks. Mickiewicz, Poland's national poet, is buried here, and a mile or so away one can climb a mound dedicated to the great patriot, Kosciuszko, and from the top of it see all Cracow with the narrow Vistula, hundreds of miles from the sea here, winding through it.

Cracow's Rynek, or market square, might almost be Venetian. A hundred yards away is Lili's, the smallest coffee shop (it may be) in the world, and they serve delicious pastry. Cracow is the only city I have ever heard of that even under a Marxist government has three times as many monasteries as cinemas.

Southward, the High Tatra and the skiing resort of Zakopane with its steep meadows rolling down from the peaks. Or, nearby, Morskie Oko, the eye of the sea, a black lake surrounded by high rocks like the rim of a volcano with snow in the rifts, even in August. Or, a little way to the west and you come to Wieliczka, the thousand-year-old salt mines, a veritable museum of carvings, hundreds of feet underground. Here also, Nowa Huta, the great Lenin Steel Works, of which more in its proper place, and not very far away the bleak, marshy waste of Auschwitz, a museum now, with almost as many tourists today as there were prisoners twenty-five years ago.

But head up toward Wroclaw and you come to Katowice. Figures are one thing. The evidence of one's own eyes is far more impressive. This great industrial complex has one of the highest per capita incomes in the Communist world, and to see it is to acquire a microcosmic picture of the entire plan, the intention, the success and failure, the vulgarity and beauty of the whole.

One goes there by train, it may be, and watches lush farmland give way to scrub and heath. Little streams begin to turn black with coal dust. Across the rolling waste men scurry about and tractors lurch along the horizon, building causeways out of slag heaps—the roads and grass-covered tumuli of tomorrow. In Poland, they tell you proudly, no waste from the mines is ever piled near inhabited places. Then, as one comes nearer to the city, chimneys as far as one can see in every direction, huge railway yards, and between the unending four-story blocks of houses, nothing except the brown, naked earth.

Katowice (like most Polish cities) has wide streets, but even the trees look sickly. The whole center of town is being knocked down and rebuilt in the interests of rational city planning. Here is a people, unlike the rest of the Poles, who do have industrial experience. They are the true working class of the country and they look it.

One has become used to slender, smiling girls with thin lips and pale, blue eyes. Here they are dark and blunt and matter of fact. One has had enough of elaborate Polish courtesy and circumlocution. Here the miners, the steel workers, the people pouring out of the textile plants work hard, drink hard, and play even harder. They have the finest football teams in Poland, are great pigeon fanciers, earn three times the national average, and are as direct and down to earth as hobnailed boots.

The city itself is built on top of an eight-hundred-year supply of good quality coal, and as a result it sits there foursquare in the midst of an industrial area thirty-six kilometers long and fourteen wide. Katowice is the smallest province in all Poland, containing only 3 per cent of the nation's area. Yet it has 11 per cent of the population, pays out 20 per cent of the wages, and is responsible for 22 per cent of total production.

I intend to talk about Polish industrialization in a later chapter, but Katowice and industry are one. They cannot be separated. So I must say here that in this tiny area there are seventy-six coal mines, sixteen iron works, a hundred machine tool factories, forty textile plants, and they intend to build factories for consumer goods too. For as they point out, they have overemphasized heavy industry. There is not enough work for the women. They are going to start a scheme, therefore, whereby housewives will be able to work during school hours if they like so they can be at home at the same time as their children.

As I pointed out above, Katowice sprawls on top of the coal, and this at a time when coal is being superseded by other forms of power. So they are going to build chemical industries here too, and convert coal into oil and plastics. In fact, to one who, like this observer, tends to be more interested in theater, perhaps, than in the production of pig iron, who would frankly rather spend three hours listening to music than ducking his way down a coal mine, a visit to Katowice had loomed up more as a duty than a pleasure. And ugly, grimy, busy Katowice turned out to be a sheer delight. It was more. In spite of error, in spite of tentative steps gone wrong, Katowice illustrates better than anything else in Poland the virtues and the advantages of economic planning. For Katowice—indeed, Silesia, is planning intelligently organized. And therein lies a world of difference.

It has a "king," Jerzy Zietek, a huge, sprawling man

who (they say) smokes good Cuban cigars, drives a
Mercedes, and can drink any man in Katowice under the
table. He fought against the Germans in the Silesian uprising after World War I. In 1939 he was a major in the
army, escaped to the Soviet Union, came back in 1944,
and battled with his unit all the way to Berlin. Now, as
Mayor, he administers his "kingdom," pokes his finger
into every available pie, and, in a government possessed
of more bureaucrats than leaders, keeps alive an almost
unique flair for cutting red tape.

"Miners need air," he says. It is not often that mines lie
directly under a city's streets. So of course if the slag is
going to be carted off into the country, the countryside
has to be brought into town. Thus, under Zietek's aegis a
park was laid out, quite one of the most wonderful in
Europe—not only with the usual walks and lawns and
shrubbery, the bandstands where amateurs can get up
and sing (to be booed or applauded), not only with an
astronomical observatory, but with seven terraced swim-
ming pools, each for a different purpose. The smallest is
for children who can barely walk. Another is for older
ones. One is for old people; near it a pool for those just
learning to swim, still another especially for those who
want to practice diving, the sixth with Olympic lanes for
racing, the seventh for general joy, with artificial waves
that come surging up for five or ten minutes in every
hour.

Katowice has five theaters, an opera house, and has
just acquired a university, affiliated with the University

of Cracow to the south. And they are proud of these things. They are proud of the fact that they produce 60 per cent of Poland's steel, 78 per cent of her zinc, and 20 per cent of her textiles. Not only this. They are bursting with enterprise and (an unheard of thing for Poland) the government have recently signed a contract to export ten million tons of Katowice coal to Japan.

Just to the west, the old German border used to cut them off from what is now Gliwice, and by 1970, they tell you, when they have finished building the Oder canal, Gliwice will be a port as large as Gdynia up in the Baltic, and out will go the coal without ever again having to be reloaded.

The whole province, for all its brashness and business and "muck is money" philosophy, is fortunate too in having a series of unusual people as its chief citizens. There is Wilhelm Szewczyk, its literary lion, the almost self-consciously elegant author of some forty books, a solid Marxist, a connoisseur of fine cigars, and a quite patrician dispenser of good brandy and conversation.

Or there is Edward Gierek, parliamentarian from Katowice, member of the Central Committee of the Party, and very much "king" of Silesia. He is not only a very shrewd politician, but a first-rate administrator too, with the interests of his constituents very much to the fore. In Warsaw, they tell you that whatever the shortages, if good nylon shirts cannot be found in Poznan, or beer in Cracow, or ham anywhere else in the country, in Katowice you will be sure to find them all.

Very few people will even dare hazard a guess as to what factions, what stresses there are on the Central Committee. But in March 1968, at the time of the student demonstrations, Gierek made an extraordinarily demagogic speech in Slask to his Silesian workers. It was far below his real level of intelligence and in it he brought out all the old Zionist plotters, the German revanchists (strange bedfellows, these), and the imperialist diehards that had to be "unmasked." A week afterward he and Mr. Spychalski, then Minister of Defense (but since promoted to be Head of State), sat beside Gomulka on the platform, and listened to their tired leader say the same things, with one serious addition—that the Soviet alliance was so much the cornerstone of Polish policy that nothing must be allowed to stand in its way. We have said Mr. Gierek is intelligent. He is also ambitious. As they say in Silesia (where he is genuinely popular), he has no sparrows in his head. It is pretty generally believed that he will before too long follow Gomulka as First Secretary of the Party.

Out in Rybnik I spent ten or twelve hours with some of the best of all, a group of miners and engineers from the Chwalowice shaft. These men all have houses, television, refrigerators, cars, for they save hard and their wages are three or four times the national average. If one says that they are paid some six or eight thousand zlotys, or in real (not official) terms about $140 a month, it sounds ridiculously low. But one must remember that their rent is barely 5 per cent of their wages, that a first-rate meal in a restaurant costs about fifty American cents, a tram ride or a telephone call a penny, that holidays are heavily subsidized, that hospital services are free. Incidentally, one is required to pay 30 per cent of the cost of a doctor's prescription. These used to be free too, but the authorities discovered that when they were not paid for they were not valued. Many prescriptions were made up and never called for.

In a word, they live well on their $140. They have good, strong, merry faces too, and an open-handed hospitality with roast goose and vodka that left me grateful, weak, and respectful of their capacities. There was Leon Wantula, for example, one of the more interesting of my companions, a miner, a novelist (Szewczyk discovered him), and a delegate to the Sejm.

"Ah," I said to him. "So you're not actually a miner, but a member of parliament."

He turned me a slightly puzzled frown. "But I went down the pit yesterday. What makes you say I'm not a miner?"

"But surely, if you're in parliament . . ."

At this he explained patiently that he was not a politician, but went to Warsaw simply to represent his constituents. How could he do this properly unless he understood their problems? And how could he understand them unless he lived and worked among them?

These men are all convinced Socialists, except that, as one of them said sadly, "People are not good enough yet for Socialism, are they?" They point to their "House of

Culture," with its stage and cinema and library, with rooms for woodworking, modeling in clay, for meetings, for stamp collectors, and heaven knows what besides. There they sing in their choir, perform operettas of their own, and plays. Their children even study ballet, and a whole curriculum of voluntary activity is scheduled for almost every hour of the week.

They have no drift from the mines as there is every-where else in the world. Conditions are too good. A man can retire at fifty-five if he likes, at a pension amounting to roughly half his wages, and if, as is often the case in Rybnik, he is a part-time farmer too, he can pretty well live on the fat of the land until the day he dies.

Brass bands, choirs, pigeons, and football, these he shares with his British, French, and German colleague. For his own he has St. Barbara's day, the fourth of December. She is the patron saint of all who work underground, having herself been immured by her fa-ther, a third-century nobleman. But while locked in her dungeon she was converted to Christianity, so her fa-ther, who had different ideas of rectitude, cut off her head.

Years ago Polish miners went to church to pray for the martyr's intercession. Nowadays the fourth of De-cember is more an occasion for sport, for music, and for celebration. But the Rybnik miner is even more inter-ested in telling you that in these same collieries before the war they brought up 69,000,000 tons a year. In 1966 the figure was a 123,000,000. As British and German coal mining decline in importance, it may well be that these Polish mines will become the most productive in Europe.

Wherever one goes in this sprawling, industrial complex one sees evidence of the prosperity it has earned for itself. On every side, new housing estates like little villages, all facing inward toward their shopping centers that are like the hubs of so many wheels.

Go west or north from Katowice and you have left the Vistula basin and reached that of the Oder. On the way to Wroclaw one passes Czestochowa, the Lourdes of Poland (except that they have more pilgrims annually than Lourdes). The dark virgin, the miracle worker, stands behind her gilded doors in the chapel there, a black-hued Madonna painted on wood, a strong, vivid, angular face. Legend has it that she was painted by St. Luke. More likely she came here from Russia with the Pauline Friars when they built the shrine late in the fourteenth century. Experts say that she is probably an eighth-century work, originally from Constantinople.

We shall be dealing with the Church in Poland later. And one should only say here that to see worshippers in Czestochowa, women in pale skirts and scarlet jackets beating their heads against the stones of the nave, to hear how when the Primate, Cardinal Wyszynski, came and the police, fearing a crush of traffic (and no doubt instructed by the Ministry of the Interior not to cooperate with the church dignitaries) forbade cars to be driven into the town, the peasants picked up Wyszynski's car and carried it into the square before the church, to see throngs day after day crowded in the little chapel for communion, people of all ages, students, shopkeepers, peasants, housewives, simply to walk through the cloisters of Czestochowa and look at the rapt, upturned faces is to discover how powerful the Church in Poland really is.

When you get to Wroclaw you are in what used to be German Silesia, but not in the quiet, provincial Breslau that was. Wroclaw is a bustling, vivid university city, half of whose inhabitants seem to have migrated from Polish Lwow in what is now Russian territory.

Like Szczecin, Wroclaw is still being rebuilt, but there the resemblance ends. For Wroclaw possesses not only a huge engineering industry; it lives in an artistic ferment greater almost than that of Warsaw itself. There are new painters, new theaters, new architects, new ideas, festivals of music, and twenty-five thousand lively and most communicative students.

It is a young city too. Only four per cent of its inhabitants are of pensionable age (Britain has three times as many), and the birth rate is more than double that of Cracow or Warsaw. It is a city of canals (there are actually more than a hundred and twenty), a city embracing a whole ecclesiastical quarter that surrounds the Archbishop's palace, a city with more green space per head of population than any other in Poland.

We shall of course come back to Wroclaw when we have occasion to discuss the contemporary Polish theater, for they are making some remarkable experiments there, and sometimes, sitting in their Artists' Club where Romain Gary and John Steinbeck have scrawled their signatures in paint across the wall, listening to scraps of conversation in Polish, French, Russian, English, answering their eager questions—"Is John Osborne doing anything? Do you happen to know Thom Gunn?"— sometimes in Wroclaw one begins to feel that it is we who are the insular ones and they a small, turbulent, eager center of the world.

Northwest again and you have almost come full circle, for you are in Poznan on the Warta, the site of the annual trade fair and in a sense Poland's gateway to the West. Poznan is a dull place, not unattractive, with wide streets and trees, a few baroque houses, some pleasant gardens. Yet the people look drab compared to those in Warsaw, plump and turgid compared to those in Wroclaw. One misses the bubble in the air, the youth, the enthusiasm. But Poznan is busy nevertheless. Here are the great Cegielski engineering works. In Poznan they make railway wagons and farm machinery, ball bearings, processed foods, ships' engines, soaps, cosmetics, and heaven knows what besides.

If the theaters cannot be compared to those in Wroclaw, they will tell you instead about the "Poznan Larks," their own choir, or about the Wieniawski competition held there every five years, in which prizes are awarded not only for composition and performance, but also for the manufacture of violins.

A group of partisans somewhere near Lublin in 1943. "They sallied out to steal weapons for Poland/And the wind made up a song about them as they marched."

Capture of a German during the uprising. Scene: the center of Warsaw. Time: September, 1944.

The burning of the Warsaw ghetto, 1943.

A *lapanka*, or street round-up, in Warsaw. People were arrested and sent to concentration camps or used as laborers in Germany.

Jewish police getting their orders just inside the ghetto wall.

Krystyna Trzesniewska—prisoner number 27,129 at Auschwitz. (*Panstwowe Museum of Auschwitz*)

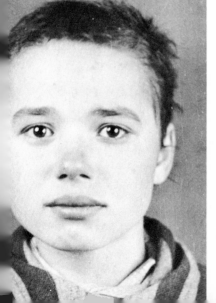

Heinz Reinefarth and other officers in Warsaw, 1944. Reinefarth is the officer wearing the Iron Cross.

The return to Warsaw. Nowy Swiat, January, 1945.

Warsaw—the market square of the Old City, 1945.

The market square in the Old City, 1968.

The junction of Marszalkowska and Jerozolimskie, Warsaw, 1945.

The same intersection in 1968.

The Vistula and the Poniatowski Bridge from Czerniakow in South Warsaw.

Arab horses at the stud farm in Janow Podlaski.

Jan Sobieski's Palace of Wilanow just outside Warsaw.

Wild bison in the forest of Bialowieza.

Katowice—muck and money—ugly but alive.

A new power station in Turoszow. (*Tadeusz Rolke*)

Fields near Rzeszow in the Southeast. Each narrow strip is a separate holding.

Mechanization in a mine near Katowice.

Mechanization on a state farm in the Poznan region.

New housing—cramped, efficient, and quite clearly prefabricated.

The Church of the Assumption of the Virgin, Wladyslawowo, built 1957–1961.

*The Labyrinth*, a production of the Tomaszewski Pantomime in Wroclaw. Costumes by Krzysztof Pankiewicz.

Zygmunt Molik in the *Akropolis* of Wyspianski. The Laboratory Theater, Wroclaw.

Jerzy Kozlowski in *The Gown*, a play based on Japanese legend and produced by the Tomaszewski Pantomime in Wroclaw.

Witold Gruca and Barbara Olkusznik in a ballet pantomime, *Mandragora*.

One of the moving sights in Poznan is the cemetery for British pilots who either died in captivity or were brought down by Germans near there during the war. Strange to see on that Polish hillside shaded with young trees, name after English name—Flying Officer Hepworth, Squadron Leader Pugh—neat crosses and grave after grave cared for by local schoolchildren.

One of the grandiose sights, on the other hand, is a vision of planning gone wild. They are digging a veritable grand canyon to change the course of the river, to make a city of what was originally a fortress, to give Poznan (God help us) promenades. In Poznan in the great crypt of the Cathedral they say Mieszko I, first king of Poland, is buried, and his successor, Boleslaw, who happened also to be the uncle of King Canute.

But the city's raison d'etre for the west is the International Trade Fair. They have put up long, white buildings to contain permanent exhibition stands. In 1967 there were forty-six nations represented, and half a million visitors. Here, they point out, is the great junction for the economic blocs of East and West, for Comecon, EFTA, the Common Market, and the United States.

Poznan is the center too for some of the finest agricultural land in the country. For Wielkopolska is a neat, fertile landscape, green, gently rolling, with tiny clumps of trees on the hilltops that rest the eye. The Manieczki State Farm near the village of Srom, for example would be a model farm anywhere in the Western world, with its workshops, its feed dryers, its creamery, its 6500 large white pigs, its 40,000 hens, its almost 5000 tuberculin-tested Friesians.

But we shall be looking more closely at Polish farming later on. With Poznan, with Manieczki we have come back almost to where we started, for from there it is only about two hundred miles up the Warta and the Oder to that northwest corner, Szczecin and the Baltic.

It would not do to finish a geographical survey of Poland, however, without at least a word about War-saw. We have talked about the bullet-pitted houses, and as we said at the very start, there is, indeed, something sad about the city. It has not, it never had any of the real beauty of Prague or Vienna or Budapest, perhaps be-cause the nineteenth century passed it by.

And although the Warsovian has a certain flair, he lacks the quiet self-confidence of the Austrian, the Hun-garian, or even the Czech. He has been battered too often. Indeed, as one of them said to me, "If you have been knocked down eight or ten times, you hesitate be-fore you stand up yet again."

We have talked about the wide streets, the clanging trams, the trees, and a great deal about the horror that befell Warsaw. But it is only in Wola that that horror is still visible. Before the war it was a joyless quarter of red brick buildings five and six storys high, and today streets like Zelazna and Chlodna simply look bleak with ruins. Here and there a new cement shell going up, but mostly it is ragged stumps of buildings like half-drawn teeth, with their tops battered and only their ground floors usable, with weeds and rubble still piled in the quondam courtyards and drab old women sitting on benches in the afternoons, faces lifted into the sunlight.

In Wola people are pale and thin. In Wola one sees drunks lurching out of doorways in midmorning, and hears their wives shouting imprecations from behind broken windows. Far up on other crag ends of houses there are balconies with the railings actually ripped away and unreplaced. There other old people sit with nothing but flower pots as barriers, as though on unsteady bridge-heads lifted out into the unsubstantial air.

A curious mixture, the new Warsaw, the Opera, the National Theater, the many churches rebuilt as they were, the parks and gardens meticulously cared for, new trees in almost every street—and dead in the middle of town Stalin's monstrous toad with spires for warts, his gift to the Polish nation, the Palace of Art and Science, which is surely one of the largest, most tasteless, and ugliest buildings in the world.

Not half a mile away, the elegant quarter, the Bristol and Europejski Hotels where the bars are open almost until dawn for foreigners, and the whores congregate under Isa, their chief, looking for dollars. Some are middle-aged and plain as whores are all over the world. Some look like wistful Madonnas impeccably dressed, until they open their unemphatic mouths and let you hear their sad, cheap voices.

Often in Warsaw the walls are paper-thin, and one can hear the trams clanging past outdoors at five or six in the morning. But the shops are full of good things (if you know where to look). Down little back streets there are dressmakers. Everywhere, papers, periodicals, reproductions of Van Gogh and Cézanne, bookshops with books in any one of six or seven languages.

The Stare Miasto has been rebuilt, as we said before; it seems more part of the city organism than does any part of Gdansk. The enchanting little Lazienki Palace was never destroyed in the first place, only gutted, so that now it stands in its park very much as it did before, like a delicate and very miniature Trianon. There on the walls, the Polish kings and queens, Jan Sobieski with his fat, patrician belly and good-humored mustaches, Casimir the great, like some Biblical dispenser of justice surrounded by adoring peasants.

There the portraits of the fine and noble families. Anna Broniarek, who knows a great deal about Polish painting, took me round one day. "Look at the women," she said. "Once a generation, goading the men on to rebellion, and for the next fifteen years they wear black veils."

Just on the outskirts, the great, provincial and yet strangely original palace of Wilanow with its bas reliefs on the outer walls and the huge, silent park that surrounds it. Or a little farther out into the country, Zelazowa Wola where Chopin was born, a tiny adjunct to a country estate with its six small rooms, the piano, Chopin's (the boy's) drawings on the walls, and outdoors the park again where on summer evenings people sit in the thousands under the trees to listen to music, where in wintertime the snow lies still and deep and rooks caw restlessly in the high branches.

In the outskirts too, on every side of Warsaw, the trim, tight, red brick vegetable farms whose owners are without any doubt the richest men in the country. Elsewhere in the world one judges a farmer by his granary. Here there are no granaries, only field after field of beans or peas or cabbages, with the whole family out carrying hoes or baskets. Every morning the wagons go creaking in to the big hotels in Warsaw. These people sell for cash (and not even the tax collector knows how much). Their granary is the Narodowy Bank, and if there are only two cars to a family it is to prevent the authorities from making an intelligent guess as to just how much they have actually hidden away.

And this panorama, from Szczecin on, this is the face of Poland. It grows, it develops, but it does not change, and in the midst of the almost endless variety there are three most important things that are happening.

First, there is the huge industrialization, with its failings and its virtues; second, there is a long-overdue revolution (just beginning) in agriculture, and third, an intense and almost silent struggle between a strong, authoritarian Communist government and a strong, authoritarian Catholic Church. We shall now look at those three facts of Polish life, and in that order.

# 9. Industrialization

Now, if at the end of a war you are going to try to lift a destroyed and impoverished nation up by its bootstraps, to industrialize ruins overnight, you are going to have to plow back every available penny into plant and manufacturing capacity. To do this you will have to keep wages abysmally low, and there is going to be a terrible lack of consumer goods. In fact, a whole generation is going to be asked to pay for the comforts of its children and grandchildren. If to do this becomes a matter of principle, if economic theory, in short (no matter how soundly elaborated), becomes more important than the people for whom it is put into practice, the people will object to the theorist.

Thus in the early days after the war the government enforced a certain degree of collectivization in agriculture and as a result, the peasant, in mute rebellion, simply sat on his hands.

[ 150 ]

By the same token, the planners tried to industrialize in all directions simultaneously. Factory wages were almost ludicrously inadequate. So there were student demonstrations, protests everywhere (except in the newspapers), and in 1956 (a positively revolutionary move) two delegates from the Cegielski engineering plant in Poznan were sent up to Warsaw to ask for higher wages. They were ignored. A second delegation followed, threatened that unless something were done there would be a hunger march, and the government was so incredibly blind as to have them arrested.

So the march took place. A ragged army of Polish workmen sallied out into the streets. Some stormed the Poznan radio station. Others broke into secret police headquarters and, in the street, pumped petrol out of cars to use it to set fire to them. Foreign newspapermen came hurrying in from Warsaw and Berlin with headlines already dancing in their heads about revolution in Communist Poland.

The question on everybody's lips that week was, "Where is Gomulka?" Wladyslaw Gomulka, who had been a wartime hero, had been in conflict with Stalin, and who had been under house arrest, was the only man everyone trusted to apply a certain common sense to the interpretation of Party ideology. Overnight he became First Secretary of the Party, had his dramatic confrontation with Khrushchev (when Poland might very well have gone the way of Hungary) and there were immediate reforms. He began his long, long balancing act between the Russian interpretation of Marxist theory and the Polish reality of popular demand. Collectivization was abandoned. Wages were raised. A certain attempt was made to get consumer goods into the shops—and the revolution was over.

But industrialization went on, simply with slightly different priorities. One of their main problems was that with the exception of coal they had remarkably few raw materials. Before the war there had hardly even been such a thing as geological research. But after 1946 the geologists went to work, and in 1953 they had their first real success. Professor Stanislaw Pawlowski discovered huge deposits of sulphur in the Tarnobrzeg region and later in the southern part of the province of Kielce. In 1958 copper was discovered too, in southern Silesia. By this time, of course, the new industrialists were beginning to see light at the end of the tunnel. In 1965 they began building the enormous fertilizer plant at Pulawy, and by 1970 it will be turning Carpathian natural gas into 6500 tons of urea and ammonium nitrate a day. This, they hope, will save the $200,000,000 they spend abroad every year on wheat.

In 1945, as we said above, their only capital was coal. Before the war most coal fields had been worked by a single shift, and Poland had exported 11,000,000 tons a year. By 1956 they were doing triple shifts and exporting 26,000,000 tons.

Men and girls came in by the hundreds of thousands from the farms. "Better a semi-productive factory worker," they will tell you, "than a redundant farmer." Textile factories, like coal mines, were put on triple shifts, each working a forty-eight-hour week, and as much of the national income as was feasible was reinvested in production. This was a terrifying burden for the economy to bear, but over and over again they hammered home one clear line of reasoning. You cannot begin to earn without production. You cannot produce without building factories. Factories require railways and railway sidings, water, electric power, roads, sewage plants, and above all, housing for the people who work there. The cost of building a power plant is great enough. The costs of the whole, complicated infrastructure are enormous.

Of course cities grew too. Cities grew, built theaters, bred poets, and developed new and unpredictable kinds of societies. New kinds of people, in fact, and unexpected forms of protest.

But for the moment we are talking about production, and perhaps some clear, cold figures showing what has been achieved would be useful (see p. 154).

So it was well into the 1950's before Poland even equaled her prewar production. For it took years, of course, before new plant and new equipment could be brought into use.

If Katowice is one of the most lively places in all Poland, there are others which in their own different ways are a bustle of activity too. Up in the north, in Gdansk, a nation that had not even a seaport fifty years

### PRODUCTION OF BASIC COMMODITIES

|  | Unit | 1938 | 1945 | 1955 | 1965 |
|---|---|---|---|---|---|
| Coal | 1,000 tons | 69,395 | 26,916 | 94,500 | 118,800 |
| Coke | " | 2,300 | —— | 10,000 | 14,400 |
| Iron ore | " | 1,098 | 175 | 1,699 | 2,861 |
| Crude steel | " | 1,961 | 650 | 4,426 | 9,088 |
| Zinc | " | 107 | 43 | 156 | 190 |
| Lead | " | 20 | 5 | 39.7 | 41.4 |
| Cement | " | 2,487 | 401 | 3,813 | 9,574 |
| Sulphur | " | —— | —— | (1958) 5 | 2,959 |
| Artificial fertilizers | " | 502 | 119 | 286 | 739 |
| Woolen yarn | " | 50.2 | 7.8 | 52 | 65.5 |
| Cotton yarn | " | 90.5 | 15 | 115 | 187 |
| Electric power | Million KWH | 7,964 | 4,489 | 17,641 | 43,774 |

ago is now building ships for export all over the world. Not only this. It has built a fishing fleet of some 165,000 tons, and brings in catches from as far afield as Labrador and Angola. In fifteen years it has doubled the number of its ships and quadrupled the weight of the fish it brings into port.

The fishermen up there form a quite individualistic society of their own, and in the very few years since the war have already built themselves a tradition. But the Poles are chiefly proud and not a little excited by their shipyards, for this is an industry built up out of nothing, with no experience to fall back on at the start, no trained craftsmen, no designers, not even the subcontractors which every shipbuilder needs before he can go to work.

On the sixth of November 1948, they launched the *Soldek,* an ore carrier—the first seagoing cargo vessel ever built on Polish soil. Then, with tramps and general cargo ships, trawlers, and steel fishing cutters they gathered know-how and experience. Tonnages increased. Technical designs were improved. In 1955 they built their first ten-thousand tonner, and by 1960 Poland was in fifth place in the world in numbers of ships completed. Today she is building over 200,000 tons a year and selling fishing vessels even to Britain, Ireland, and Norway. Now they are planning to double that output, and talking about their first 150,000-ton tanker.

One point they stress when they show a visitor around is the youth of their labor force. Stocznia Gdanska employs some 16,000 men, of whom a third are under twenty-five, and only 13.7 per cent over forty-five. There are girls too, mostly electricians, and several of them far prettier than one normally expects an electrician to be. In addition they run a technical school for shipbuilders, with eight hundred pupils aged fourteen to nineteen. Here at least, the technical expertise most of Poland lacks is being drilled into a whole new generation of workmen.

Every nation of shipbuilders has its specialty. Thus the Japanese are known particularly among the cognoscenti as designers of rudders. The Poles are modestly proud of their own condensers and electric motors, and in fact, their two great handicaps so far are the inferior work done by some of their subcontractors (particularly when they are trying to compete for foreign orders), and a lack of experience among their workmen in welding the new, thin steel.

But here in Gdansk, in Szczecin to the west, and particularly in Gdynia (where there is more room, geographically, for development) Poland is building an industry which, if it grows as they plan, will eventually provide very serious competition for the British, the Germans, and the Japanese.

Shipbuilding, sulphur mining, copper and aluminum, all these are new. In 1966 a new aluminum plant was opened in the province of Poznan, which will eventually double production. Only in steel do they have no expectation of any real increase, for Poland lacks iron mines. So in 1966 they produced 9.2 million tons of crude steel, about as much as the Canadians, and with that they will have to be satisfied for the foreseeable future.

But in Pulawy, about seventy-five miles up the Vistula from Warsaw, another and entirely different kind of industry is growing. This is the Azota works, the nitrate plant being built on a sandy stretch of land that was nothing but pine and scrub two or three years ago.

They work hard and efficiently there, but they pay no attention to the amenities, the salesmanship, if you like, which would make an equivalent plant in Germany or America, with its board room, its elegant offices, its charts on public view, its palm-fringed reception rooms smell of success and profitability.

But such frills never come within "the plan." By the same token, incidentally, Polish advertising is almost ludicrous. On some major roads one sees huge billboards bearing the face of an almost cadaverous woman and the legend, "Polish cosmetics for you." Or in Krucza in Warsaw, in the center of the tourist belt, there is a large window displaying Polish farm products, and in English in large letters up above, the words, "Buy Polish egg." Or on the road to Lodz one reads so often that one should "Buy Polish marine paints" that one makes a silent promise never to do so if it can possibly be helped.

At Pulawy, which is one of their industrial show-places, the stairs are narrow. The offices are small. The areas between buildings are like a blasted heath on which someone without any luck at all has tried to grow a lawn. But it is what they do there that counts. It is Pulawy's place in the rational overall plan that is impor-tant. And it is Pulawy's task to supply nitrates for 50,000 hectares of land a day.

Now, of course, mixed fertilizers are compounded of equal parts of nitrates, phosphates, and potash. Potash will be produced in the German Democratic Republic (or what we call East Germany). Phosphates will come from imported phosphate rock. And Azota will produce 60 per cent of Poland's nitrates. By 1970 they expect to save the cost of two million tons of imported wheat a year.

Much more important, they hope to raise the general level of farm productivity and put it on a par with that in the west. In 1966, for example, the Poles used seventy-two kilograms of fertilizer per hectare. The Dutch used five hundred kilograms, and therein lies a world of difference. Incidentally, Poland is a country of light, sandy soils that need not only chemicals, but humus. Azota will therefore not be a cure-all, and they know it—simply a long step forward.

We talked before about the infrastructure of industrialization, and this of course includes housing. I said in a previous chapter that most of the new housing seemed to me unbearably drab, cramped, and unimaginative. I am told (although I have no positive evidence) that architects are emigrating in their hundreds every year because the bureaucracy puts so much red tape in their way and talented designs are so often passed over in favor of the functionally commonplace that they have lost all heart.

For pure functionalism has become the watchword, functionalism plus a maximum of economy. Party officials will tell you that it is not bureaucracy which has discouraged architects—rather the reverse. The state has accepted thirty or thirty-five designs for buildings which can be prefabricated. No other housing at the moment is permitted to be built. Furthermore, the law lays down that space shall be allocated at the rate of six square meters per person, which means in fact that the new blocks for workers, say, at Nowa Huta, the great steel works near Cracow, are vast rectangles composed of innumerable paper-thin boxes. Around them, nothing but the naked earth, for landscaping is an unnecessary frill when one is building in a hurry.

You drive up from the mill, and there stand the upright sugarlumps far too close to each other, all the same color of wet cement. The flats themselves are minute, of course, but what is far worse, they are shoddily made, with plaster that flakes before it is really dry, doors and windows that do not fit.

But, as one man said who had just moved in, "It looks uncomfortable, but you ought to see what we used to have. The workman doesn't know his job—true. But things are improving. Today in Nowa Huta, a third of the labor is doing twice the work that was done here fourteen years ago."

On my insistence that bad workmanship was not relative, that Poland was too poor a country to build blocks of flats that would simply have to be torn down and rebuilt in ten or fifteen years, he simply smiled, asked his wife to bring us coffee, and explained (as I had heard it explained a dozen times) that people cost more than cement. If in a certain number of years they had to rebuild, well and good. In the meantime, people would have had a place to live.

Others of us there did not agree. The mutual friend who had brought me argued heatedly that this generation was supposedly paying for the comfort of the next. But the next would have to pay all over again to make up for the slovenliness of its fathers.

The neat little wife came in with cake, coffee, and cherry brandy. "People!" she cried. "All he talks about is people because he's a crazy idealist. Do you know why any work at all gets done in Poland? The bosses work for the accountants, the foremen work for the norms, and the men on the floor do what amounts to three days' work a week and expect a productivity bonus."

Her husband listened, smiled patiently, and said he thought otherwise. Workmen had to learn. They were not experienced enough yet for Socialism, and too inexperienced to take any pride in their work. After all, ten years ago the mason was a peasant boy who had not even learned to read.

It was an argument I had heard many times, and indeed it is largely true that because of the enormous shift of population (and a migration from the farms to the cities) a large, untrained labor force has come into being. And since Socialism holds that every man has the right to work (trained or no), the semiliterate country boys and girls have been given tools and foremen and turned into plumbers, carpenters, machinists, and boilermakers, sometimes with disastrous results.

It is thus part of the story of Poland's industrialization to say that far too often workmanship is simply bad. By the same token, service in the shops is abominable. And the expert, the Party member, will agree. Always the same answer. "What do you expect?" they ask. "The girl's just arrived from a farm in Bieszczady. She still thinks you need matches to switch on the light." Or they will explain that in the new, democratic Poland, to serve others is considered degrading, so the waiter is rude and wears a dirty coat simply to prove that he is as good a man as you. Or, if they are being a bit more honest and more accurate, they will tell you that wages have risen far too slowly and provide no real incentive, so (as many Poles have had to do for almost thirty years) a man will have to fiddle something on the side to make ends meet.

What they will never admit is that because of the lack of competition there are rarely incentives to do any more than one must, that in most factories ten men do the work of six, and that if a man should be discharged for sheer idleness or incompetence or drunkenness, all he has to do is cross the road to find another job. Marxist teaching insists on every man's right to work, but it says remarkably little about his obligation to work as well as he is able. It forbids us to profit out of another man's sweat. But nowhere does it forbid competition in service or amenity or design or quality. In fact, however, the current generation of Polish party theoreticians is so afraid of deviation from what it considers orthodoxy that it has become far more conservative than the founding fathers themselves.

Until now, Socialist norms and targets have generally been quantitative. If the goal is ten million pairs of shoes and the ten million have been produced, it has not been politic to ask if the shoes are well designed or handsome or tasteful or in the current style. If you make two blades of grass grow where one grew before, the planning commission announces that grass productivity has been doubled, but it never asks if it is good quality grass. Today, however, the seller's market in Poland is almost over. Everybody has shoes, and now, predictably enough, they want better shoes.

Not only that. If Poland is to export consumer goods (as she wants very much to do) she must do so in competition with the highly industrialized nations of the west. That the government are aware of the problem and seriously concerned about it we know from a report late in 1967 by Stefan Jedrychowski, chairman of the planning commission. He has discovered that mass employment has brought far higher incomes per family than wage rates would normally suggest. An employee today supports only 1.2 people instead of the 1.5 he supported only seven or eight years ago. This has meant that there is more money in people's pockets than there are consumer goods to spend it on. As a result, Poles are consuming fifty-two kilograms of meat a year per capita, and that is as much as the Swedes eat. This means not only that there is less meat to export. The cost of imported feeding stuffs rises.

So what has the Socialist answer been? To raise the price of meat. In other words, suppress demand instead of correcting the imbalance that created the demand in the first place.

But as the report says, "Public needs are changing. Today people require goods of better quality, of a higher standard, more modern and more fashionable than our industry is yet capable of producing."

Socialism has many virtues, but it has a built-in defect too, that it requires a state planning commission to tell it the obvious. To be sure, Mr. Jedrychowski points out, today is better than yesterday (this has come to be something of a Polish saying). Standards of consumption have risen beyond the wildest dreams of twenty years ago. Today in Poland, he says, there are 104 television sets to every thousand families, 42 refrigerators, 150 washing machines, 62 vacuum cleaners, 50 motorcycles, and 236 radios.

By western standards (one radio to every four families) these figures are of course not extraordinary. But if one remembers where Poland started at the end of the war, the achievement is worthy of respect.

And (all carping aside) that is probably the point. In spite of errors, in spite of the fact that central planning magnifies any miscalculation, sometimes to a calamitous degree, in spite of the lack of training, of incentive, of individual sense of direction, in spite of a positively stifling bureaucracy (the dry cleaner fills out a form in quadruplicate and without carbon paper to help), in spite of public lethargy and a lack of governmental initiative, in spite of the straightjacket of political dogma and the positive dread of either responsibility or originality, Poland has so far achieved the degree of industrialization that she planned for herself. Foreign loans would have helped (she has had very few). A huge influx of foreign capital would have put the country on its feet far more rapidly. There has been no such influx. She has lifted herself up by her own bootstraps, more or less unaided. Her programs, her norms, have generally been exceeded.

As a result, before the war only 7 per cent of her total production was in engineering. Today it is 26 per cent. Today they manufacture their own power plants and heavy machine tools. In fact, they produce some 90 per cent of their own capital equipment, and in 1966 they exported capital equipment worth some $900,000,000 to the rest of the world.

At last, they will tell you, they have reached a point where they no longer need to make up for the past. But to produce in ever-growing quantities for the future they must overcome several basic difficulties. They must, for example, increase foreign trade, particularly with the West. Here they have certain very definite problems which we shall come to in a moment. Even so, the prospects are not bad at all. In 1958, exports of goods (as distinct from services) amounted roughly to one billion dollars. In 1967 they exported almost two and a half times as much. From 1939 to 1967, exports of manufactured goods (as opposed to agricultural produce) rose from 7 per cent to 50 per cent of the total, and with new plants, indeed whole new industries annually coming into production, they expect to increase this proportion considerably.

It might be interesting at this point to set down a few specific figures to put Polish foreign trade into some sort of perspective. As we might have expected, the greatest proportion of her exports to Eastern Europe go to the

Soviet Union, of those to Western Europe, to the United Kingdom.

As far as the Eastern bloc are concerned, some 50 percent of their total exports go to the USSR. They sell chemical plants, excavating equipment, plywood, and sugar refining plants, machine tools and railway carriages. From the Russians they buy 78 per cent of their iron ore, and they feel (at least at an official level) that their trade with the Soviet Union is to mutual economic advantage. Second and third in the list of their Eastern trading partners are Czechoslovakia (to whom they sell machine tools) and the German Democratic Republic.

About 65 per cent of Poland's foreign trade is with Eastern Europe. Most of the remainder is with Western Europe and the United States.

To America the Poles sold $87,000,000 worth of goods in 1967, more than half of it foodstuffs. The rest was clothing, willow products, furniture, glass. And the interesting thing is that they have a favorable balance of trade with the United States, and for three reasons. Public Law 480, which regulated the sale of agricultural surpluses, has been repealed, so that whereas between 1957 and 1964 the Poles bought half a billion dollars' worth of grain from America, these sales have now ceased. Second, the United States will not permit sales to the Eastern bloc of computers or of certain other technical equipment which Poland (for one) would very much like to buy. Third, the Americans will not grant to Poland the long-term credits for the purchase of capital equipment which are normal commercial practice between nations. And it is not as if Polish credit were at fault. The Poles have always paid their debts dead on time.

No, it is part of the American anti-Communist crusade which the Poles look at with uneasy sadness. They desire peace so ardently—and they do have experience of war —that it is difficult for them to understand a powerful nation (with a large Polish minority) which insists on maintaining so ineffectual a state of economic hostilities.

They tell a tale about the Firestone Tire Company. It seems Firestone was about to sign a contract to build a tire manufacturing plant in Rumania. But such a hue and cry, such a boycott against Firestone was started in America for "selling to the Reds," that the plan had to be abandoned.

Trade with Britain is a far happier story. It amounts to 20.4 per cent of all Poland's trade with the West. And for the British, there is a debit balance, gradually diminishing. Thus, for the past three years, Polish exports have risen, but their imports have risen even more rapidly.

|  | 1965 | 1966 | 1967 |
|---|---|---|---|
| Polish exports to Britain | £48.5m | £53.7m | £56.3m |
| Polish imports from Britain | £24.3m | £35.1m | £48.5m |

Some 60 per cent of these Polish sales were of agricultural products. Thus in 1967 there were 54,000 tons of bacon, 19,800 tons of butter, £80,000 worth of cheese, £500,000 worth of eggs, and £460,000 worth of beef and poultry. Textiles, including ready-made clothing, came to over £800,000, toys to £200,000, shoes to £750,000, and pharmaceutical products to £120,000.

They want to buy British goods in ever larger quantities, but they complain that the prices are not competitive. After the 1967 devaluation, ICI put its prices *up* by 16 per cent (according to Polish government economists), and wool, which after all, had no foreign cost increases to absorb, went up in price too. For purely emotional reasons, they would like to increase trade with this "biggest partner." The only thing that stands in the way is Britain herself.

Above all, they would like to extend coproduction with the West. They know perfectly well that they cannot compete either in quality or in price with the West's vast industrial giants, vast not only in their capacities, but in the markets they control. But they have bought the rights to manufacture Fiats in Warsaw, and with Italian technical help will manufacture cars of Western quality to sell in their home market. Or, to take another example, they have bought a license to manufacture Grundig tape recorders. Already their engineers have worked out a method of improving one of the models—and this improvement has in turn been sold back to Grundig.

Coproduction of this sort would not only, they feel, be of mutual benefit, it would bring new techniques and a new sort of discipline into Polish factories. This, in turn, would increase the quality of their own manufactures, and thus their opportunity to build trade with Western Europe. To turn the Eastern and Western blocs into mutually interdependent economies would be one of the surest ways of ensuring peace in Europe. Conversely, to allow them to grow into competitors for the still undeveloped markets of Africa and Asia would bring about a situation which has in the past frequently led to war.

Growing economic intercourse means that the Poles must by every means possible increase their production of raw materials. Over the past ten years they have a little more than trebled their production of such commodities as cement, copper, brown coal, coking coal, natural gas, almost doubled per capita output of steel and plastics, whereas the rise in production of such commodities as sulphur and refined oil has been even higher.

As for manufactured goods in heavy industries, the figures are just as interesting. Take a few products almost at random, and the production figures turn out not only to be increasing, but doing so at an ever-accelerating rate.

These figures, which it must be admitted are impressive, were achieved during a period when they claim to have had an acute shortage of labor. If they had said a shortage of skilled labor one would have agreed even more strongly. But two things have happened to help solve that problem. First, the Poles are at last beginning (as in the Gdansk shipyard) to see the necessity for building a trained labor force. And second, in the early

## PRODUCTION IN HEAVY INDUSTRY

|  | 1950 | 1955 | 1960 | 1965 |
|---|---|---|---|---|
| Diesel engines | 1,200 | 4,500 | 4,100 | 12,200 |
| Electric locomotives | —— | 7 | 38 | 72 |
| Steam locomotives | —— | 91 | 144 | 319 |
| Electric rotating engines (1000's) | 76.6 | 201 | 1,108 | 2,077 |
| Ball bearings (millions) | 0.5 | 3.5 | 12 | 34.1 |
| Road building machinery (tons) | 3,600 | 16,800 | 35,300 | 47,000 |
| Combine harvesters | —— | 300 | 564 | 1,781 |
| Textile spinning machines | 340 | 555 | 1,557 | 2,468 |
| Textile weaving machines | 1,020 | 1,559 | 3,275 | 3,882 |

1950's they experienced a positively explosive baby boom. The facts are hard to accept in the West, but Polish sociologists are unanimous in calling it an unconscious reaction to having been slaughtered during the war. The figures are startling. Thus, per thousand of population the number of live births in Poland and in its Western contemporaries varied as follows.

|  | 1950 | 1955 |
|---|---|---|
| Great Britain | 16.3 | 15.5 |
| Germany | 16.5 | 16.0 |
| France | 20.7 | 18.6 |
| United States | 23.5 | 24.7 |
| Poland | 30.7 | 29.1 |

So in a nation that has risen from twenty four million in 1945 to thirty-two million today, about 40 per cent of the population is under twenty years of age.

We have said they want to increase foreign trade and the production of raw materials. They want also to increase industrial cooperation. Thus Polish woolen blankets might be dyed in Hungary, bound in Germany, and exported to France. Or food that used to be delivered raw might (after the purchase of certain foreign patents) be processed and canned and thus sold at a far higher price than before. Incidentally, purely because it is both unexpected and interesting, they now sell between five and eight hundred tons of snails every year to the French.

And we said last of all that they plan to modernize what they have built since the war and to strive for quality as opposed to mere quantity. For they feel that if they succeed in a qualitative improvement in manufactures their rate of growth can be maintained. Since 1950 production has multiplied sixfold. Real wages (*pace* Mr. Jedrychowski) have grown far more slowly. But now, with the coming to age of a new generation more fully trained, and thus a large increase in the working population, it looks indeed as though the Poles will raise their standard of living (and in the very next few years) beyond anything they have ever before imagined. Only two things seem to me to militate against this possibility.

First, the amount of self-delusion that looks to be a part of all Marxist societies. If one points out that we in the West have our own delusions, the fact must be admitted. The American government never told the truth about the war in Vietnam. The British government never told the truth about Rhodesia. The government of De Gaulle never even told the truth about itself. But a Socialist society that purports to be based on a rational analysis of economic forces (as opposed to political forces) must (by definition) see clearly and be seen to see clearly if it is to be believed. If it does not, its whole *raison d'être*, its whole justification for depriving people of certain economic and political liberties, has disappeared.

Second, they seem unable to improvise and to strike out in new directions that have not been foreseen. One talks to their planners. One looks at the perfectly reliable figures put out by their Central Statistical Office, and in no time at all even an amateur economist is able to perceive that they are juggling figures to prove what they want to prove. Not falsifying (they are both too honest and too intelligent for that), but using tonnages, percentages, hectares, or numbers of people in a way best calculated to illustrate the virtues of Marxist economics.

They will tell you, for example, that they plan for a growth rate of over 8 per cent a year, and this is of course an impressive figure. But they will be unable to quote a figure on which the 8 per cent is based. Or they will present statistics to make it plain that they are catching up with the more heavily industrialized nations of the West. But out of their own mouths they contradict themselves.

Andrzej Karpinski, one of their foremost economic planners, has published a short and authoritative pamphlet on the Polish economy.[1] Mr. Karpinski has one of the shrewdest, clearest minds it has ever been my good fortune to meet. But among other things, he compares production in Poland and the West to illustrate his point that Poland is catching up with her competitors. Thus he quotes figures for three major industrial products as follows.

| | 1938 | 1963 |
|---|---|---|
| *Steel Production* *(millions of tons)* | | |
| U.S. and Great Britain | 39.4 | 123.0 |
| France, Italy, Germany | 29.0 | 59.3 |
| Poland | 1.4 | 8.0 |
| *Electricity Output* *(1000 million KWH)* | | |
| U.S. and Great Britain | 176 | 1,154.0 |
| France, Italy, Germany | 67 | 306.0 |
| Poland | 4 | 37.0 |
| *Cement Production* *(millions of tons)* | | |
| U.S. and Great Britain | 26.1 | 73.8 |
| France, Italy, Germany | 20.0 | 69.1 |
| Poland | 1.7 | 7.7 |

He points out therefore that Polish steel production is almost six times as great as it was, its production of electric power nine times, and its production of cement over four times the prewar total. Using this proportional

[1] Andrzej Karpinski, *Twenty Years of Poland's Economic Development, 1944–64*, Warsaw, 1964.

measuring rod, Western Europe and America have not done anywhere near so well. He does not point out that the reason is simple, that they started from entirely different bases, that the West was already heavily industrialized and that he is simply playing tricks with arithmetic. And this, not because he is less able to do arithmetic than the rest of us, but because he is tied to the wheel of a doctrinaire chariot and makes his prescribed number of somersaults with no more than the vaguest idea in which direction he is going.

Or he will list production figures for a host of lesser products and show that Poland's proportionate share of these manufactures is greater than it was. This is no doubt true, but it certainly does not substantiate his claim that Poland is catching up with the West. Indeed, on the basis of the aggregate figures quoted above, she seems actually to be falling farther behind.

And indeed, so long as their standard of living is reasonably comfortable, what difference does it make? America has piled up material goods without, I think most Americans will agree, being made particularly happier thereby. American prosperity has always been the envy of the crowded poor, of those who had nothing as the Poles had nothing. Today the prosperity of the United States might as well be that of another planet so far as they are concerned. It is unreal and beyond envy. Indeed, if there is one nation whose institutions and way of life they respect and would like to emulate, it is probably Great Britain.

Mr. Karpinski is on much solider ground when he reports the improvement in Poland's diet as evidence of her vast increase in productivity. Thus today they are actually consuming more butter per capita than the Americans, more milk and sugar than the French or Germans, and their consumption of meat, while it does not yet equal that of all Western nations, is more than three times what it was before the war.

In a word, the Poles have pulled themselves up a very long way by those bootstraps of theirs, and they have every reason to be proud of the fact. They were hungry and got food. They were homeless and built houses. If their experts twist facts, trying to prove that they have done better than in fact they have, perhaps it is understandable. For ten or twelve generations, Poles have lived surrounded by neighbors who told them they were worse. Perhaps they even began to believe it of themselves.

There is another fact that ought to be taken into account in assessing Poland's chances for the future. They are a highly intelligent and talented people. But for two hundred years, ever since the partitions of the late eighteenth century, Poles who wanted to make any mark in the world (indeed, very often, Poles who simply wanted to survive) had to do so abroad. Thus most of the great Western nations—from Australia to France, Britain, and America—have large Polish minorities. From Kosciuszko to Chopin, from Marie Curie to Conrad, Feliks Topolski, and even Roman Polanski, great and talented Poles have generally been exiles. With every new Polish catastrophe, the wars, the ill-fated uprisings, the defeats, there was a great wave of emigration. No nation can afford to have its best and bravest forever leaving home.

Today they are permitted to travel—and many of them do—to England, to America, to France. But when they have earned enough hard currency to buy the Mercedes and Cadillacs which are the Polish status symbols they generally bring them back. Even the politically unhappy tend to feel that their roots are Polish, that they could not really be happy anywhere else. If the Poles stay at home, then, and if their production continues to increase (as it shows every sign of doing), and if the ideologists, the adherents to the dogma that knows only truth and lie, correct and incorrect, but nothing in between—if they grow old and give place to their juniors (there are already strong rumors that this may happen), then Poland's future looks very bright indeed.

Whether the old guard likes it or not, economic change is coming, if only because it makes plain common sense. Otherwise they simply will not be able to satisfy demand. If they do not, there will be dissatisfaction. This, in turn, will have to be met with further measures of repression—and probably, as a result, with a drastic slowing down of the rate of economic growth.

In a word, *their* variety of economic orthodoxy is going to have to be abandoned. There is going to have to be a measure of decentralization, and market forces are going to have to be respected a great deal more than they have been until now. There will be political changes too. Whether these changes will make for liberalization it is still far too early to say.

We have talked, albeit briefly, about industry. But half this nation still lives on the land, and that is a very different story indeed.

# 10. The Farm

COMING IN from the west by air, the first things
one notices are the variegated fields as narrow as pencils
lying tightly side by side between the quiet rivers. And
that first view from the air is distinctively Polish, because
for hundreds of years now the land has been split into
smaller and smaller segments as it kept being divided
among heirs. Today the strips are often no wider than
three long paces from side to side, and this is of course
not an economic size if one is going to use motorized
equipment, or indeed even if one works with a plow
and horses. It was only in 1963 that a law was finally
passed, forbidding the subdivision of property into units
of less than about sixteen acres.

Then, coming down to land at almost any Polish city,
sweeping over cultivated stretches at six or eight hundred feet, it strikes one that the growth is patchy, as
though fertilizer had been scattered hit or miss, without

any system. At ground level, on the other hand, one sees immediately that it could not be Western Europe or America, but for quite a different reason. The hedgerows are a mass of wild flowers, the glades alive with pale green beetles and butterflies of every conceivable color. Even before dawn the bird chorus begins as it used to do in England, while after dark the owls swoop softly down and young, unfrightened rabbits come out amid the corn.

In a word, there is no spraying of pesticides, so the natural relationship of field and rivulet, larva and bird, insect and flower, the mutual interdependence of small beasts has never been disrupted. That is one reason why the Polish countryside is so unexpectedly lovely to look at.

The little "brooks too wide for leaping" are clean because there are no detergents to flow into them. Poles who come home from abroad now and then try to improve this sad state of affairs. One young girl who visited us in England took back a suitcase full of whiter than white bleaching powder, some bottles of foamy washing-up liquid, ten dozen Brillo pads, and twenty-four dozen packets of chewing gum (for these things excited her by their novelty), so in time Poland too may hope to enjoy what she obviously thought the best in Western civilization. For the present, her streams are still unpolluted, her hedgerows still uncluttered and innocent, her insects, hares, voles, and field mice still not considered enemies of progress.

The Polish peasant, like peasants the world over, is devoutly religious, politically conservative, and innately suspicious of both strangers and innovations. In many parts of the country, in Bieszczady, for example, or in Bialystok, it is doubtful if anything about him has really changed in two hundred years. Eighty-three per cent of the land is owned by people who constitute only 11.8 per cent of Party membership, and those figures tell a tale that needs no comment.

Thus the Socialist government found there were two problems they would never be able to solve satisfactorily without enormous patience. One was their relationship with the Church, the other with the peasant who formed the Church's staunchest pillar. At the end of the war they expropriated the large estates and turned them as well as some smaller holdings into collective farms. But collectivization was not only immensely unpopular; it turned out to be an economic failure. So ten years later Gomulka was forced to revoke it. Now, a dozen years later still, faced with very serious agricultural problems indeed, the government are gingerly starting to modernize one of the most backward farming communities in Europe.

There are four kinds of farm properties in Poland today. By far the greatest proportion, some 83 per cent (or about three and a half million farms) are privately owned and managed. These average 4.8 hectares, or about twelve acres each. Many are obviously far smaller. A man may own two or three tiny patches of half a hectare each at opposite ends of a village, and this continual subdivision over the generations has kept Polish agriculture limping farther and farther behind that of its Western contemporaries. Like many other troubles inherited from the days of partition, it is most prevalent in the areas once administered by the Austrians and the Russians, that is, in the southern and eastern parts of the country.

About 15 per cent of agricultural property is organized into state farms such as the one we looked at briefly in Wielkopolska near Srom. These state farms are of really viable size. They average about six or seven hundred hectares, and the men who work them do so on salary under a manager and assistants who are normally graduates of agricultural schools. What they produce is sold to the government, and indeed crops like flax or sugar beet could never be sold anywhere else. One ought to add at this point that profits from state farms have so far been very low, for they have had enormous sums to pay off in original investment for both housing and machinery. But as in industry, their establishment is part of a long-term plan to rationalize the whole agricultural system. And already the plan is beginning to bear fruit. From 1961 to 1965 state farm production increased twice as fast as did farm production in all the rest of the country.

One per cent of all farmland is still organized in collectives, and as a matter of fact agricultural experts in Warsaw will tell one today they are glad the proportion is so small. "Think of the overtime we'd have to pay for getting the harvests in," they say. "A farmer who does it on his own land does it for nothing." One can only reflect what a pity it is they have not realized this is true of other forms of self-employment too.

The fourth kind of farm property is that which has been organized into what they call peasant circles, almost a halfway house between private management and the collective. The peasant circles are groups of small farmers who have banded together voluntarily, been given government loans, and therewith bought machinery and equipment which no single farm unit is large enough to use economically.

Now in the course of only three or four years some ten million people moved from the countryside to the towns, often leaving elderly parents to work the farms on their own. A government survey in 1967 discovered that a large proportion of the most poorly managed—and thus the least productive—farms were run by people sixty years old or older.

So wherever they can profitably do so, the authorities are taking these properties over. In the winter of 1967–68, three new laws were promulgated and passed to regulate such takeovers.

A peasant of pensionable age may give his property to the state, providing it is larger than five hectares and can without too much difficulty be made part of a state farm. He is allowed to keep one hectare, plus all buildings and farm equipment. In addition he is given a pension which varies according to circumstances, but must not exceed that of a normal worker. The government estimates this will bring in some 200,000 hectares a year. No gift of land, no pension is the rule, for as they frankly admit, they are more interested in raising farm productivity than they are in the welfare of the individual peasant.

A peasant may, on the other hand, sell his land to the state. Indeed, if he is grossly inefficient, he can be forced to sell. The money he receives is put to his credit in a banking account, and may thereafter only be used for agricultural investment, to buy equipment, for example, for a peasant circle.

Land may, of course, be inherited as heretofore. But the inheritor must be a bona fide farmer and work the land himself. If he does not, the transfer is void and the land is taken over by the state.

And third, there was a ruling of a more technical nature, concerning the unification of small properties. The purpose of all this is of course to enlarge the units of cultivation, thus permitting mechanization and the rotation of crops, to eliminate some of the five million hectares devoted to footpaths between tiny properties, and slowly to get rid of the greatly inefficient minuscule properties.

Among state farms, Manieczki, near Poznan, is one of the showplaces, and it is laid out on a positively princely scale. There lie five thousand hectares of gently rolling land, 94 per cent of it arable, with its own streams and roads and with neat cottages for the six or seven hundred workmen who live there with their families. They even have communal dining rooms that serve a multiple purpose. The men, who of course have no cars, would find it awkward to go home—perhaps several miles—every day for their lunches. So the farm kitchens feed them hot meals instead of the bread, pickles, and salami they would normally carry, and their wives, not having to prepare a meal in the middle of the day, can spend a few profitable hours, if they like, in the dairy or the henhouses.

Unlike some other farms I saw, Manieczki even on the surface appears to be well run. Pleasantly enough, they keep about sixty horses, mostly used for getting from place to place across the fields, and wherever one looks, planning and good management have gone into the lay-out and equipment. The long, cool, pig and cattle houses have narrow-gauge railway tracks running from door to door to make both feeding and mucking out easier. Unlike any privately owned farm I ever saw in Poland, they have mechanical milking, their own creamery, and are of course able to keep the meticulous records of litters and egg production, of milk yield and butterfat that a farmer must have if he is to breed his stock successfully.

Hay and silage they have aplenty, and machine-dried lucerne which they export to the Swiss and the Italians. Being so large a unit, they can afford their own machine shops too. In fact, they form their own small community, almost entirely self-sufficient. And where had they found the laborers? From among landless peasants whose families had emigrated to the towns or whose holdings, perhaps, had shrunk by reason of that endless subdivision until they were no longer going concerns.

Whatever the case, they lived well. Wages were not high, but in compensation there were overtime earnings. The food was good. The cottages were tidy, with bean rows and flower gardens. Like any prosperous Western farmers, they scuffed the dust in the roads, talked crops, and rode their tractors or their combine harvesters all day across those rolling fields under an unimaginably blue and distant sky.

Other state farms I saw were not nearly so idyllic. At Pierkunowo near Gizycko, for example, they produce seed for the four principal grains and potatoes for vodka. They keep about four thousand Redpoll cattle and eighty-five workmen, all to take care of about 2300 acres. At Pierkunowo the yards looked sloppy, the stalls old-fashioned, the pigsties filthy and unswept. Here and there by the roadside or even in the farmyards themselves lay bits of untended machinery, and the fields looked ragged after the grain had gone, as though they had been worked by a harvester whose blades wanted sharpening.

At Garbno they had neat cow stalls, freshly painted, but a plague of flies enough to make Pharaoh tremble, flies in greater numbers than I have ever seen them, flies clustered like swarming bees in the rafters overhead, flies that got into one's eyes and nose and mouth, that were even crushed underfoot as one walked.

The manager was young, redcheeked, had just been given his degree in agronomy, and was very anxious to be helpful. The flies even swarmed in his office, and he knew all about DDT, heaven knows, but that affected the milk and the feed. There were other sprays, but they were poisonous to the animals. And one felt in a way that he represented in microcosm the whole of Polish industry, eager, willing, doing wonders with the tools he had at hand, but simply not aware of the enormous technological resources available to his Western equivalent.

On far too many of the Polish farms that I saw it is accepted as a fact of nature that a hen will lay about seventy-five eggs a year, or that yields per acre are normally far lower than the Western farmer expects. This is of course inefficiency. By the same token, cattle are almost invariably Friesians (because of their huge yields) or Redpoll (because they produce both milk and beef). But Guernseys and Jerseys seem not to exist. Experts have propagated the myth that the Polish climate is unsuitable. Nor does one see Holstein or Hereford or Angus steers. For as in industry, they are still going for quantity and not quality, and this is, at least in my opinion, a mistake (repeated in almost every field of production) that will have to be put right before this nation can really come into its own.

One thinks of Poland as an agricultural nation, and of

course this is true, but not nearly so much as formerly, when 65 per cent of her people lived off the land, for now the proportions are about half and half. The strange thing is, however, that for a nation devoted to agriculture, although her rainfall is normal, averaging about 700 mm annually, she has comparatively poor soil. To be sure, there was an area of black earth near Lwow, but that went to the Russians. Now the best farmland lies between Gdansk and Bydgoszcz, in the Poznan area, and around Wroclaw. Some two-thirds of the country is covered by what they call a "bleached soil," thin and sandy. There the only crops that grow really well are rye and potatoes. That, of course, is why the Poles have eaten rye bread (and not white bread) ever since they ceased being a nomadic people. And the huge quantities of potatoes served with every meal may have something to do with the fact that Polish women are too often corpulent long before they reach middle age.

To make matters more difficult, the mean annual temperature is only 44°F., and this makes for a short growing season. Even worse, large areas of farmland are inadequately drained and irrigated. But in spite of these handicaps—and the greatest of all is (as we have seen) the minute size of individual holdings—Poland is self-sufficient in all basic farm products except wheat, and she even exports large quantities of livestock. If, therefore, any real improvement can be made in production—and output was increased by some 14 per cent between 1964 and 1967—it will not only provide for their own growing population, but earn them hard currency as well.

The modernization of industry is more or less on the way to being accomplished. The modernization of agriculture is a far more difficult task which they have now set themselves. For they not only have the vagaries of the weather to contend with and a shortage of humus in the soil. They are trying to modernize the most individualistic and indeed primitive of all human enterprises, and they are trying to do it without allowing the entrepreneur to buy up large and economically viable acreages, invest capital in machinery, and farm these areas intensively and for a profit.

To reintroduce the *kolkhoz*, or collective, would cost the country far too much for it ever to be considered in the foreseeable future. Not only—as we said before— would they have to pay overtime wages for work the private peasant now does of his own free will. Not only would they have to equip the collectives with modern machinery (and this might be the equivalent of building a whole new railway system), but like the balance of nature, the balance of an economy cannot be altered except at the risk of sometimes unpredictable dangers that might get quite out of hand.

To take a simple, a quite elementary example, let us postulate an area of two hundred and fifty hectares which the authorities decide ought to be farmed collectively. This area will be the property of perhaps fifty families. They will live in fifty houses, have fifty stalls, byres, barns, perhaps a hundred horses.

Fifty families are a hundred and fifty people, but only twenty-five or thirty will be necessary for the running of this planned collective. So the rest will have to be found work, and not only work, but new houses and schools. They will need electricity, a water supply, a whole new infrastructure somewhere away from the farm. Not only that. These people who are used to country customs, who speak country dialects and wear country clothes, will have to get used to a whole new way of life.

Millions, of course, have done just that. The drift toward more comfortable jobs and houses in the cities, toward film and television and fashionable clothes, and lower middle class pretensions has grown and become a veritable flood. So much so that the government has had to step in and (just at a time when they need more industrial labor) limit the numbers of migrants by establishing quotas for both housing and work in the cities.

Such are the headaches of planners. The shift must and will continue, for not only are there still far too many people on the farms; there are far too few in the cities. But unless there is to be chaos, the change must be ". . . still in strictest measure even" to the allocation of work, housing, utilities, and natural resources.

And yet, as one agricultural expert said to me, no plan is ever accomplished without a hitch, for in the long run human ingenuity will overcome any bureaucrat's quota.

A peasant wife looks after the animals. She wakes at four to do the milking and feed the cows and horses. Then she makes breakfast for those going out to work, gets the children off to school, feeds the hens, collects eggs, milks the goat, and sets the goat's milk out to sour for cheese-making. Then by the time she has made up the beds and cleaned her kitchen it is time to do the midday milking. And so her day goes by with chores indoors and out so that often she is the last one in the family to go to bed— just after her husband has stumbled home from the wine shop. And her daughter? Her daughter grows up in this environment and once a month goes to a film. That is enough. By the time she is fourteen she has decided that she would rather die than marry a farmer.

"So she moves into the town," one interlocutor said, "goes to work in a shop—never wore shoes in her life except on Sunday—and you and I complain that she doesn't know her job."

As with everything else in Poland, history made both the farm and its peasant proprietor what they are today. And this with their variety, from the derelict bits of land near Szczecin to the narrowest pencil strips of all near Bialystok, from the warm, snug little valleys south of Lublin to the great, rich properties east of Poznan.

For the two hundred years of partition, government was the peasant's enemy and the Church his friend. Then came six years during which no man ever knew if he would be alive by nightfall—and now, being a devout Catholic, he is again in opposition to authority, and so much so that if the Ministry asks him to sow wheat instead of corn, rye in place of barley, he is as likely as not to do the opposite. Indeed, one of the problems the planners at Pulawy face is that they will have difficulty in convincing the peasant that fertilizers can increase the weight of his crops. They are thinking of subsidies, sales of fertilizers linked with other commodities, even the purchase of horses so that less grain will be needed in the first place.

"But the peasant needs his horse," they will tell you, "if for nothing else, to make a show as it takes him to church on Sunday."

And sadly they will remind you in Warsaw of Marx's prophecy that Communism would come first to the heavily industrialized nations. He postulated a trained labor force that would be able to take over and manage both the farms and the factories. In Poland, heaven knows, they were not trained, not even industrialized, and certainly not prepared.

The worker must be taught to use a lathe. The peasant must be taught to drive a tractor, to rotate crops, but as far as the authorities are concerned, there will be no attempt at compulsion. It would defeat its own ends.

Instead there will be the slow redeployment and training of labor, the gradual buying up of farms and turning them into larger units, organizing them under managers who are not entrepreneurs, but agricultural experts.

It is a laborious, complicated, and very long-term

project. The pity of it is that the Church could be of enormous help, for she has great influence among the peasants. But the Church is not lifting a finger.

The Roman Catholic Church is a force that has rarely been satisfied to be neutral. And by the same token, few of us in the Western world have ever been neutral to its teachings. Yet let it be said at once that except to the purely theoretical Marxist, the story of the Church in Poland is enormously complex. And because it is so closely allied to the peasantry, I propose that we look at it now.

# 11. The Church

To BEGIN WITH, nobody knows just what proportion of Poles is devout or goes regularly to Mass. One Party official said to me, "Older people? Yes. But the younger generation belongs to us."

On the other hand, Professor Stomma, representing the right-wing Catholic organization, ZNAK, points out that the Church is the only real power in Poland outside the Party. According to him, 80 per cent of the people are avowed Catholics and 98 per cent have their children baptized. In fact, he goes so far as to say that the massive industrialization has made the Church even stronger, for the worker whose whole way of life has changed with his removal from the land to the city turns to the priest who is his only link with the past.

Other less biased observers offered widely varying estimates of the Church's power. They all agree that the vast majority are churchgoers. But Church and Party are not by any means mutually exclusive. I met churchmen who are Marxists as well as sincere Party members who with equal devotion go to Mass. Very early on it becomes plain to any observer who tries to remain unprejudiced that the split between the religious hierarchy and the political theorists is both unnecessary and in the long run actually likely to be healed.

To begin with, the priesthood is very much part of the sinew of the nation. Between a quarter and a third of all Polish priests were murdered during the war. There were priests among the partisans, nunneries that took in Jewish children, and in the concentration camps priests came second only to Jews (and about on a par with Communists) in the savageries to which they were subjected.

I doubt if there is a village in all Poland without its church or where the priest is not very much the person of his parish, as well as being mentor, psychiatrist, lawyer, judge, jury, and decider of all questions between heaven and earth. So to wipe out the influence of the priesthood in Poland would be a moral as well as a physical impossibility.

The authorities, anticlerical though they may be, are perfectly aware of this, and although they have expropriated a certain amount of Church land, they have in the main showed a spirit of tolerance which, with some justification, they wish might more often be returned.

Thus the war cost Poland as great a proportion of its churches as it did buildings of any other sort, and in the first twenty years after the Germans were driven out, close on a thousand of these were rebuilt. Some were of course reconstructions or major repairs. Others are quite literally breathtaking and original, and belong among the finest examples of modern European architecture. There is, for example, the magnificent Church of the Assumption of the Virgin in Wladyslawowo, designed by Messrs. Baum and Kulesza and built between 1957 and 1961. Or there is the beautiful little church of the Virgin of Fatima in Tarnow, built in 1960 by the three architects, Jozlowski, Seibert, and Wolak. The Church of the Elevation of the Cross in Roj, designed and built by Augustyniak, is a structure of startling strength, and has in it modern glass set in concrete, lighting and even contemporary frescoes (depicting the stages of the Cross) not only moving and delightful, but very much a product of our time. No one who has seen Janina Schmidt's stone *Christ in Distress* in Gdansk is likely to forget its powerful impact, or the Christ slumped hanging behind the altar at Nowe Tychy. Things like these make the familiar baroque look commonplace. They bring the Church right into the heart of the twentieth century.

And even Cardinal Wyszynski has paid tribute to the government for its assistance. At the consecration of the reconstructed Cathedral of St. John in Warsaw, he said, "Fairness demands that I express my thanks to the state authorities who, particularly during the rebuilding of the walls, provided experts, advice, and assistance, for they were fully aware that this was a matter of saving one more monument of a national and religious culture."

This, from the state's bitterest enemy, is praise indeed, and of course the help of an anticlerical government was not given without strong, but subtle pressures having been applied. The first such was naturally the mute desire of the vast majority of the people that the work be done. No Polish government, unless it wished to divorce itself entirely from the will of the governed, could afford to ignore the wishes of the ecclesiastical authorities. But second, and perhaps no less strong, is the almost universal longing among Poles for the reconstruction of their national identity, with its language, its literature, its history, and above all with physical evidence on every side of both its roots and their survival. The countless churches rebuilt in their former styles, and with a fastidious attention to architectural detail were reerected for exactly the same reasons that Gdansk and the Stare Miastro in Warsaw were reerected, and for the same reason that battered Germanic facades in Wroclaw were sometimes demolished. Poland not only had to be rebuilt. It had to be seen at the same time to have had a glorious past.

To do this they worked with many sorts of materials. There are churches of stone, of brick, of concrete, lath and plaster, and (particularly in the Cracow region) even of wood. And perhaps because they were not built in quantity, and plans never had to satisfy anyone except the church authorities, they are often full of a vivid imagination and a willingness to experiment with new techniques.

Furthermore, these churches are living and breathing organisms. The services held in them are crowded, not only with old people as the Party would have one believe, but with the young as well, not only in the country, but in the towns. In any university city it is by no means unusual to see students in jeans and miniskirts kneeling in the church vestibule because they have not been able to find room to kneel in the nave itself.

Now, as I said at the beginning, the relationship between Church and state is a highly complicated matter. Just as the peasant was traditionally opposed to the partitioning power, so was the worker opposed to his employer. Today the employer is the state, the authorities are Socialists, and no matter what those authorities may do, the initial reaction will be conditioned by that traditional spirit of opposition. But with the Church there is an added complication. The Polish Catholic Church owes its allegiance to Rome. Socialism has been imported from the Soviet Union, and Russia is not only an old enemy. She is the heir of Byzantium, and Byzantium was not only a political, but a religious enemy too. Religious antipathies die hard.

As one man said to me (in a positive fury) in Warsaw, "Go to Lwow. Go across the Bug and you will see without any question that you have crossed a frontier. The houses, the peasants, the churches, the very look in their eyes—everything is different. Poland is one world.

Russia is another. And they don't even know over there how miserable they are, for they've never been allowed to be happy."

His was the first generation, he maintained (and he was in his middle forties), that had been born consciously Polish, that had had an operative government and not simply a romantic dream to guide them. For these people, devoutly Catholic, radically nationalistic, and within living memory freed from foreign masters, Byzantium is and always will be anathema. And yet, to confuse the issue even further, patriotism in Poland had always been a left-wing phenomenon, for the right wing traditionally supported the partitioning power.

So the reaction of any one individual to both Church and state is not altogether conditioned by either his politics or his religion, but by an amalgam of both, compounded with his geographical, social, and educational background, as well as with his own particular ability to free himself from the automatic reactions generated by over a century of shibboleths.

Thus Marx referred to religion as the opium of the people at a time when employers (as they do in Spain and Portugal today) used the Church as a means of suppressing political opposition to change. And conversely, the Church has always felt itself to be a bastion of civilization against Marxism so long as the left wing seemed to be attacking the property on which so much of its own temporal power was really based.

In Poland today these attitudes no longer have any

bearing on the situation. The clock is not going to be turned back. The ruling ideology may have been imported from beyond the Bug, but it is not in the foreseeable future going to return there. The Primate, Cardinal Wyszynski, stands like a monolith (or, as he might prefer it, a harbor light) with the tide of history sweeping out past him. But he is no longer defending the rights of property, simply the past. And conversely, the First Secretary of the Party is not so much at war with the Polish Church as with the intransigent old man who until 1967 was alone at the head of it. Mr. Gomulka is reputed to have said that he would not object so much to Wyszynski if His Eminence would only abide by the decisions of the Vatican Ecumenical Council.

But the Vatican is older than either of these old antagonists. In May 1967, the Pope changed the status of the four bishops in the western territories that used to be German. They were made apostolic administrators, which brought them directly under the Holy See instead of under the Primate. In June of the same year another step was taken with the creation of a second Polish Cardinal. This was Archbishop Wojtyla of Cracow, a young and vigorous man who began his career little more than twenty years ago as a worker-priest and who today has become the best visible hope of an eventual rapprochement between Church and state.

I tried on several occasions to meet and talk with Cardinal Wyszynski, who enjoys a huge and unquestionable popularity among the masses. He was not willing that I do so. Polish and Western diplomats alike agree that he has latterly become almost entirely unapproachable. One churchman told me that His Eminence had even gone so far as to refuse audience to a notable Dutch Catholic who had presented letters of introduction from several Dutch bishops.

But I did spend an hour with Cardinal Wojtyla in Cracow. Unfortunately he received me only on condition that I not print anything he said. Not that he had anything to hide, or wished our talk to be confidential. No, he felt (and I must say, with some justice) that what we talked about was so complex a matter, the whole relationship of Church and state in Poland had so many ramifications, that whatever one quoted him as saying would be bound to be a simplification and only one facet either of the truth or of what he would wish to say about it. He is a warm, witty, shrewd, and persuasive individual with a quickness of mind quite equal to that of his political opponents. I do not think I shall be betraying a confidence if I say that when I met him he was busily reading Marx.

Elsewhere in Cracow—and later in Warsaw and Lublin—I had occasion to meet and talk at some length with Polish Catholics of several political persuasions. They are divisible roughly into three groups, and among them elect a total of thirteen delegates to the Sejm.

To the far right is ZNAK, which publishes *Tygodnik Powszechny* (or *Universal Weekly*) and a monthly, *Znak* (*The Sign*), in Cracow. As far as they are con-

cerned, Socialism is an unwelcome *fait accompli*, a geo-
political necessity. They would like, among other things,
a rapprochement with Germany, a "mutual forgiveness,"
for to them the Church and the Church alone is a reality,
past, present, or future. In a word, they want to create
ties at almost any cost with the West. According to
them, political ideologies and perhaps even national
boundaries are merely ephemerae.

The center group is the Christian Social Association
(CHSS) which seems to be relatively without influence.
To the left stands PAX, and while its adherents are as
ardent Catholics as anyone else, they nevertheless claim
to accept Socialist economic changes as being both
proper and desirable. We shall come back to PAX in a
moment (there is an extremely interesting story attached
to it) for as with most other things in Poland, its reality
is a far different thing from what it appears or from
what one is first told about it.

ZNAK like to think of themselves as an intellectual
elite. They hold meetings and discussions in many cities
and have a particularly friendly relationship with the
Polish episcopate, for the bishops too feel certain reser-
vations (to say the least) about the political changes that
have taken place. To them the Church is a fortress in a
Socialist sea, and the seventy or so bishops normally
present a united front—at least, in public. But that there
are private political differences between them is pretty
generally known.

Wyszynski is of course still the dominant figure. His

opinions are rock-ribbed and so far as one can see, unalterable. He will accept change in the West. As a matter of fact, he will accept liberalization anywhere in Europe. But he will not accept Socialism in Poland, for there, he says, the church is not free. And by free he means free to express itself as a political force, for that it is free in religious matters I think no one questions.

In a word, Cardinal Wyszynski feels that he has been called upon to play the role of ecclesiastical disciplinarian, for his is a paternalistic society, an island round which the sea of faith (*pace* Matthew Arnold) still flows. Since Stalin's death, according to him, the whole Socialist camp is in a state of disintegration. And indeed his supporters will maintain that he is really a political neutral. He is no friend of capitalism either, only of the traditional social teachings of the Church that hark back to the safe, sane worlds of Pius XI and Pius XII. Ideally, they say, he would probably like to live in a Utopian Catholic environment, perhaps one more or less similar to that of Salazar.

In this, of course, he is to the right of the Vatican Council, and even of ZNAK. As one churchman said to me, "When John XXIII told us that a window had been opened, Wyszynski's first thought was to slam it shut before any fresh air could get in."

It is in PAX that the best hope ought to lie for eventual peace with the secular forces. For while PAX accepts the rational inevitability of Socialism, they want to broaden and develop it, to introduce a certain multiplicity into Socialist thinking. The true Marxist expects social, political, and economic forces to act and react according to the tenets of Marxist dogma, for Marxism has a monopoly of the truth.

PAX disagrees. Socialism may be a historical fact and here to stay, but they feel one can be a Socialist without being a pure Marxist, that without variety there is death, that as things are going today they are as likely to reach chaos as Communism, but above all that a belief in God and in pure Marxian materialism are quite incompatible. There is no predetermined date, they feel, for the halting of philosophical evolution, and the publication of *Das Kapital* had nothing about it like the sound of the last trump.

So far the theory. But now let us go back for a moment to a few odds and ends of fact that begin by seeming to be utterly irrelevant. But bear with me. They are fact nevertheless, and they lead to certain unexpected conclusions.

In the 1930's a young man appeared on the scene in Warsaw, personable, ambitious, intelligent, and a great womanizer. Normally no mention of any man's sexual proclivities would really be proper in what purports to be serious history. But for once I think it is justified, for in this case it quite literally saved the man's life.

He was Boleslaw Piasecki, and he first came to notice when he worked as a journalist on a rag called *Prosto z Mostu*, or *Straight Off the Bridge*, the implications of the title in Polish being greater than meet the eye.

Piasecki had money, women, and political ambitions. He wrote articles for the Fascist paper, *Sztafeta*, and eventually (in 1934, when he was barely twenty) founded an extraordinarily nasty right-wing party called the Falanga with its own uniforms, its own weapons, and its own fighting squads who attacked Jews in the streets. The war came. Piasecki fought (albeit briefly) for Poland, but by October 1939, he was back in Warsaw trying to make contact with certain Wehrmacht officers —for what purpose has never been made quite clear.

That same month, probably because he proved too much of a Polish nationalist for their liking, the Gestapo had him arrested and sentenced to death. It was then that a woman called Gawronska, who was passionately devoted to him, bethought her of certain connections she had in Italy. An emissary was sent to Count Ciano, from him to Mussolini, and within a matter of days young Piasecki was set free.

That he had courage no one has ever questioned. He became a leader in the underground—but with the NSZ who attacked isolated units of the Red Army and are said to have hunted down and murdered certain Jews as well, after they had managed to escape into the forests from their ghettos.

By 1943 he had become so notorious that General Sikorski, then leading the Polish government in exile, ordered him to be arrested and tried by a Home Army court. This would have meant his almost certain execution. But just then Sikorski died tragically at Gibraltar, and once again Piasecki had escaped, almost as though by a miracle.

At last in 1944 he was captured by the Russians—once more tried and sentenced to death, and this should at last have been the end of an extremely unpleasant man. But it was General Serov of the Russian Secret Service, the NKVD, who was in charge of Piasecki's interrogation, and Serov had an extremely agile mind.

Here was the Soviet Union about to liberate Catholic Poland and set up a Socialist government, not only one that would act as a buffer against the West, but one constituted to further its own (the Russians') economic and political purposes. It was almost impossible to overestimate the influence the Church had on the peasantry—and yet not one single Catholic organization, hardly even a half-dozen individual priests had rallied to the cause. The Russians were about to be faced with the mute resistance of perhaps nine-tenths of a people whose religious leaders, already martyred under the Nazis, were quite ready to suffer again for saying quite openly what they thought.

What happened in Piasecki's dirty cell near Otwock we cannot say with any certainty. A certain Jozef Swiatlo, one of Serov's deputies, who defected to the Americans in 1953, has given a circumstantial account of the meetings Piasecki had with Serov. It is impossible to know whether or not he was telling the truth.

But this can be said with certainty. Within a very few months of the end of the war, Piasecki was once again free and back in Warsaw in charge of a new organization he called PAX, whose rallying cry was soon heard in its own newspapers all over the country. We are Catholic, PAX proclaimed. We believe in God, *and* we believe in the changes the Soviet Union has brought about.

It has been said that in the early days Piasecki was offered financial help by his government. He denies that it was accepted. Instead he suggested that he (and PAX) be allowed to organize a small private company or two, and this was agreed to. So he founded Veritas, and Veritas are manufacturers of all sorts of religious necessities, crucifixes and rosaries, communion wine and medallions, things no Catholic could do without and—even more to the point—things no Catholic was able to buy anywhere else.

Then there was a second firm called INCO. INCO produces cosmetics of very good quality, as well as various plastics and waterproofing materials which are used in government buildings. Even more interesting, unlike the various state-owned enterprises, neither INCO nor Veritas paid taxes until 1961.

Many old members of the Falanga, friends of Piasecki in his Jew-baiting days, are now on PAX's payroll, men like Ryszard Reiff, who exercises an astonishing amount of political power, but who thirty years ago was as ignorant a thug as his master, or, even more notoriously perhaps, Zygmunt Przetakiewicz, who is still a thug today. He had been head of the Falanga fighting squads, was for years editor of the PAX newspaper, *Slowo Powszechny*, and was only deposed when the Polish

Union of Journalists deprived him of his membership for making an impromptu, drunken, anti-Semitic speech in the Journalists' Club in Foksal. Przetakiewicz was, when last heard of, head of the PAX propaganda section.

Aside from all this, of course, PAX owns a publishing house which produces not only the work of religious writers, but a great variety of other fine authors too. On my latest visit to Warsaw I was told by several writers—quite separately—that Piasecki had lately invited them to dinner, as though he were courting respectability. Of course they had refused to go. Few people in Poland mention his name. When they do it is with contempt. For a short period during the great, hopeful thaw after Gomulka first came to power, questions were asked about PAX and Piasecki in the press. They have stopped being asked.

On two occasions I asked Party spokesmen to account for this strange, almost unreal sequence of events—perhaps to deny (if they so wished) that it had ever occurred.

One said, "You take it too seriously. We all make mistakes when we are young."

The other explained that it had been a very humane and intelligent move by the Party. Piasecki had saved many lives by convincing former dissidents like himself that further opposition was useless.

As for Piasecki himself, he suffered a terrible blow in 1957. His young son, Bohdan who, by all accounts, was an intelligent and likable boy, was kidnapped and brutally murdered. In spite of enormous publicity and the offer (by PAX) of rewards in foreign currency, the assassins were never found. Since then, they say, Piasecki has become a devout churchgoer for the first time in his life.

PAX, as an organization, has only about six thousand members, but its employees are well paid, efficient, and loyal. They sell some three hundred thousand copies of their various periodicals every week. Not a single one (so far as I have been able to find out) of the Polish bishops supports them. So that in spite of the fact that to all intents and purposes, PAX stands on the side of the future, the old stubborn Cardinal, Wyszynski, is still very much the head of the Church in Poland.

Meanwhile, down at the Catholic University in Lublin, the young men take their vows. In Wroclaw the nuns walk two by two under the trees. The priests in their white cassocks in Czestochowa serve the thousands of pilgrims at communion, and it is these thousands kneeling with rapt faces about whom all the politics are being waged. It is the peasants supine on the stones in front of a thousand altars, the people worshipping something older than Christ that cause both politicians and theologians to go through their intricate dialectical dance. For them the theories, the ideologies, the programs and speeches, the subterfuges and the downright lies, for they are the (perhaps) three-quarters of a nation who do most earnestly profess the faith of their fathers and who are nevertheless quite inextricably bound up with the success or failure of a philosophy whose teachers contradict that faith.

Any human aspiration wears down to shoddy if it rubs up long enough against political expediency. The phrase-makers, the utilitarian manufacturers of words, the builders of consensus are great men for turning tears, blood, and even the light of reason into verbiage. In Poland the antagonists are evenly matched. Party and Church are both old, shrewd, patient, and certain that both time and the truth are on their side. But as we said earlier, their quarrel is becoming less and less pertinent to the realities of the twentieth century.

The government's refusal to allow the Pope to visit Poland in 1966 for the millenary celebrations of Polish Catholicism was at best an error in judgment. When Eduard Ochab, then Polish Head of State, failed to visit the Pope when in Rome in 1967, he lost the opportunity to come nearer an eventual understanding. And this failure can be blamed on two quite different faults, one human, one political. First, there is the personal animosity felt for each other by the heads of both Church and state in Poland today. Second, and far more important, is the sheer disregard for human intelligence that the Eastern European Socialist displays when he talks to someone with whom he does not agree.

It is the same disregard, the same contempt that enables them to foist a Piasecki upon a nation,[1] the same,

[1] An only partly adequate version of the Piasecki story may be found in Lucjan Blit's *The Eastern Pretender*, published by Hutchin-

and we shall deal with this anon, that allows them to print in their newspapers that almost every reader knows to be untrue, the same that enables their spokesmen to tell a foreign observer blatant lies when it should be apparent even to the dullest among them that the lie is utterly transparent and therefore useless.

They have betrayed the ideology for which they stand and which is the reason for all their work. It is almost a form of a self-hypnosis from which they suffer, and which prevents their being able to look at these things with any objectivity. They have betrayed the hopes of their own youth, for the Gomulkas of this world began as idealists of a rare intelligence and courage. If they were simply thugs one would understand all this. But they are far from being thugs. They began by "going left," in the words of the old soldier, "in search of something in which they could believe." They became Socialists—Communists, if you will—and this was a noble thing, a humane and intelligent philosophy. But the ends can justify the means only for so long. After a while, lies and cynicism destroy the ends themselves. And then what have you left?

The Poles can only hope that new men—perhaps younger men—will act differently when the time comes. Even members of the Central Committee have been heard to mention Cardinal Wojtyla with respect. For as far

son, London, 1965. The main facts are there set down, but Mr. Blit's excitable style, his frequent inaccuracies, his failure to check sources, and a way he has of occasionally contradicting himself do not inspire confidence in what he has to say.

as one can tell he, at least, is an honest man with whom one can deal honestly. And that hope is why, as we have seen in a previous chapter, Poland has been rife with rumors for well over a year of changes at the very top of the governmental hierarchy.

Government and Church both exist for the people. If they fail to respond to the people's needs they fail in everything, and in Poland a great many Marxists and a great many Catholics are wise enough and honest enough to be perfectly aware of the fact.

# 12. Painters and Film-Makers

Artists in Communist countries have no patrons, for (at least in Poland) the only people with enough money in their pockets are vegetable farmers or currency speculators, and neither of these two categories is particularly noted for its love of painting and sculpture.

So Janina Schmidt's desolate stone Christ in Gdansk was commissioned by the Church, and Jerzy Bandura's fine monument commemorating Grünwald, by the state. Bandura is Professor of Fine Arts at the University of Cracow, a vigorous, hearty man in his fifties who put the problem of young Polish artists in a nutshell.

"They come from the villages," he said, "and they think of themselves as 'modern' and 'advanced' and in rebellion against the past. But they're only the first generation. They have no artistic pasts of their own to rebel against."

"Poland is all priorities," he will tell his visitor. "You people abroad—you want a statue so you buy one. But with us, it's a matter of building a school first, or a factory. There's an old saying that a peasant can't buy a shirt until he's sold his eggs."

He paces up and down, stops to fill the wine glasses. Around him on the walls, models of his own work, copies of Rodin, a plaster replica (made by his students) of the enchanting Nike of Paionias in the Acropolis Museum. "I want us to go our own Polish direction," he says. "Pop art—Op art—all rubbish. No bones to it. I want an art based on reality. The drop of water flows of its own free will—downstream to the sea. The finest work has to have the same free and natural inevitability about it."

And this is all very fine, but the millennium is not yet here and we must look at things as they are. We began by saying that in Poland there is a dearth of patrons. Now and then an artist has a stroke of luck and sells a painting to some enthusiastic foreigner. But foreigners are not exactly thick on the ground, so in fact there are only three ways a painter can make a living—and this, no matter how industrious or original he is. He can teach (and art schools have sprung up all over the country). He can design posters or illustrate books for a publisher (and as a result, Polish posters and book illustration are quite extraordinarily good). Or he can sell pictures to the National Gallery, and Professor Lorentz, who is its director, has proved to be a patron of extremely catholic tastes and a generous hand.

It is difficult to talk about painters and their work without using the all-too-familiar jargon of critics and dealers. To me, at least, this is a meaningless language, and I can use no other language than my own. So it would be best if I simply tell what I—who, after all, am only one observer—have seen.

Now, the Poles have a dichotomy in their natures that makes them different from most other peoples. They are first of all incurably romantic, romantic as Mickiewicz was, or Chopin or Sienkiewicz, and second, they have been horribly, brutally hurt.

And this dichotomy is reflected in almost all the serious work I saw. Their illustrations, the delicate wash drawings for children's books, are a sheer, sentimental delight. It is like ballet, all grace, all lightness and joy. Their painting and sculpture reflect this joyousness too, but ally it, indeed often intertwine it with a brutality like a kick in the pit of the belly.

Bronislaw Linke, only lately dead, left a huge body of work like a hundred-headed protest—against German viciousness in Warsaw, American viciousness in Vietnam, Communist inability to differentiate between men and machines. His ghetto walls writhe in anguish; the very bricks in his houses are in pain. A little, wide-eyed, ragged girl stands hopefully under a poster bearing Hitler's face. An old Jew wraps his prayer shawl round him, and he *is* a house in whom other people live. A thousand planes are caught in the searchlights and a house made of half-broken bricks shakes its fist at the sky.

Up in Gdansk where there is a flourishing art colony, men like Potworowski and Nowasielski experiment less with structure or even line than with color. All is pure color superimposed on memories of Klee, on memories of Byzantine icons. Or in Warsaw, Anna Gintner, who is distinctly no colorist, paints her pale, surrealist and completely asexual nudes, boy and girl, young man, young woman, sitting side by side and gazing at us quite without feeling as though they had not bodies, only minds.

Or there is Jerzy Krawczyk, whose people, half real, half shadow, drift across some lifeless marketplace and leave one with a not quite explainable sense of uneasiness. Markowski paints his romantic, pale grotesques like death and a dream all mixed in the imagination. Or Juliusz Narzynski his powerful reinterpretations, his birth of Venus, for example, after Botticelli, the face infinitely innocent and appealing behind its windblown hair, the wrinkled and naked body, white fat, and over-blown as the body of a toad.

One wanders through the summer exhibition in Sopot and there they are again, Krawczyk, Ignacy Witz, Andrzej Pietsch of Cracow, and always (though these men differ in the means they employ), always the same dichotomy, the pity and terror and beauty like a blow.

There is no such thing in Poland as "Socialist art," and not even the Party pretends otherwise. Instead, there is a vast variety of talents built on Poland's preoccupation with its own experience.

In the eighteenth century, at the end of Poland's time of grandeur, there were few painters produced, to be sure, but a whole host of minor composers who served the same purpose, the expression of that enchanting sentimentality, that wry joyousness and grace that are part of Poland's gift to the world. Men like Michal Oginski, or women like Maria Szymanowska, or indeed military heroes like Kosciuszko wrote their delightful and entirely artificial music to reflect the spirit of a delightful and entirely artificial world.

Today Andrzej Pietsch draws a wan, enchanting girl who sits in a railway carriage—and thus far, the past. But the world around her, the station, the city, the near windows are alive with whores and drunken men, with lechers and crooked crones, with the sick, the dying, the tormented, torn ticket in hatband, dead matches on floor. But a child sits there too, looking out through the window, and *her* field of vision is crowded with bright castles. In short, the Poles are not designers or geometricians in their art, or makers of form. They are, if you like, moralists.

One of the most interesting new ideas is that of a man called Wlodzimierz Borowski who had a show in Poznan in the spring of 1968. He feels we are tired of shapes, of *things*, that we no longer have any faith in final definition. No painting, therefore, no *thing* can be ultimately satisfying. So instead he composes what he calls a partitura, an orchestral score wherein the instruments are colors, movements, sounds, all transcribed onto tapes and thence projected onto the four white walls of a room through speakers and optical instruments.

And this partitura, composed of course of many parts, of an almost endless ringing of chromatic changes, can be written down in code as though one were programming a computer, this symbol signifying brightness, that, shadow, a third duration or perhaps intensity, a fourth loudness or brightness or tone—so that the next "conductor," reading the code, can reinterpret it and, like the conductor of an orchestra, give old notes or sequences new meanings.

Wherever one looks one finds fresh ideas, and only one thing can be said about them with any certainty. There is variety, there is individuality, there are good and bad, but there is nothing tawdry, because unlike some of the rest of us, they still take these things seriously. One remembers the wistful bronze wolf in front of the Artists' Institute in Warsaw, the hackles rising on its back (for wolves are by definition ferocious), its jaw slavering. But the poor beast is pigeon-toed. Or the stone lions that face each other across a gateway in Krakowskie Przedmiescie, the saddest, most woebegone and ridiculous lions that one has ever seen. That is Polish art, never ethereal, always self-mocking and by means of that mockery trying to laugh away the needle burning in the brain.

It is perhaps characteristic of the Poles as a nation that

in the most lighthearted of arts, namely the dance, there should be a vast difference in quality between what springs out of the peasantry and what is descended from classical tradition. Folk dancing is a serious art, practiced by many hundreds of village groups. Every September the vast stadium in Warsaw is crowded to the rim for the harvest festival where one may watch dancing of really magnificent precision, color, and variety.

By the same token, woolen rugs, individually designed and woven, skirts, capes, wood and silverwork, glassware, all of very fine quality and made to traditional designs, come from the peasant cooperatives. They far surpass factory products and are correspondingly expensive.

But Polish ballet cannot be compared to that of the Danes, the Russians, or even the Germans. There is only one dancer of stature, Stanislaw Szymanski, and one ballerina, Barbara Olkusznik. But, astonishingly enough, these two are not only superb classical dancers. They are devotees of Martha Graham too, and in a ballet like *Samotność* (*Loneliness*) to the music of Augustyn Bloch perform a contemporary dance with as much power and precision as one would expect in New York.

It would not do to write about the Polish visual arts without at least a word about television. The Warsaw studios are minute, grubby, old-fashioned, and must be enormously inconvenient for both artists and cameramen. To be sure, they tell you, new studios are in process of being built. A second channel is being started in 1968. Color will come a year afterward. And there are two programs and two programs only which no director would ever dare cut. One is a speech by the First Secretary of the Party; the other is a football match.

I watched a rehearsal of *Crime and Punishment* one morning, and it was directed by Adam Hanuszkiewicz, their *enfant terrible*, who also played Raskolnikov. For the technically minded, there were only three cameras on the floor, one of which seemed never to be used (it was being held in reserve). The studio was about forty feet by twenty-five. The lighting was almost primitive, and the cameras, ranged side by side, alternated long, long close shots of whoever was speaking (never what is known as a reaction shot) while Hanuszkiewicz interrupted his own and others' scenes to shout directions.

"Mix!" he shouts, "Mix!" in the middle of one of Raskolnikov's tirades.

"Not yet," comes a voice from up in the control room.

"Mix! Mix! Mix!" he bellows. And meanwhile the scene goes on. Assistants crawl round on hands and knees during the dialogue, painting marks at actors' feet. Photographers crouch and circle, taking snapshots from every conceivable angle. Cameramen shout for more light. Hanuszkiewicz argues. "Silence!" somebody cries out, but it is really *Alice in Wonderland* and nobody pays the slightest attention.

An improvisation, a theatrical production in front of

cameras, yet somehow it pays off. A few hours later a really rather moving production goes out on the air. Hanuszkiewicz, himself, is very fine, and suddenly one feels sad that our own studios, with ten times the money and equipment, rarely give us more than a certain tired competence.

Among all the visual arts, however, the Poles have made their mark most noticeably in films. Warsaw has done its share, chiefly of documentaries and shorts. But most of the real work has come out of the first-rate film school and studios in Lodz.

Now, in general, when a Pole wants to explain some facet of his work, he starts by giving one a lecture on Polish history. And probably he is right, for in Poland very little is understandable except by reference to the past. Thus, the first thing one is told at the studios in Lodz is that for two hundred years the nation's real leaders have generally been the artists. After the nineteenth-century rebellions, the positivists, after World War I, Paderewski. And after Hitler's war it was Polish films that first told the world clearly and with remarkable acuity just what the nation was feeling.

The history of the Polish cinema during the past twenty years is worthy of a book by itself, and we can offer here what is at best no more than a cursory glance at the subject—first, because it is so small a part of the current Polish scene, but more important, because we are looking at Poland as it is today—in 1968—and the great period of Polish cinematography is at least for the time being at an end.

As did everyone else, the film-makers in Lodz started work after the war, caught up in an obsession with the war itself. Those awful years had somehow to be documented, explained, analyzed, the bitter experience chewed over and over in an attempt somehow to come to terms with it.

Thus, the first major film to come out of Poland after the war was Wanda Jakubowska's *The Last Stage* in 1948. The script was written in collaboration with the German, Gerda Schneider, and proved to be an almost documentary study of life in the women's barracks at Auschwitz. Today it already seems remote. In 1948 it must have had a horrifying impact, restrained, objective, clinical, and thus all the more real.

At the same time Aleksander Ford brought out his *Border Street*, a story about children and war, children and the ghetto. In 1950 Jerzy Zarzycki produced *Unvanquished City* (Warsaw, of course) with a fine script by himself and Jerzy Andrzejewski, who was to do even finer work a decade and more later.

It is interesting, incidentally (and it will be a familiar story to Western writers) to learn that *Unvanquished City* began as a script called *A Warsaw Robinson Crusoe*. It was Andrzejewski's own story about a man who had survived the uprising in 1944 and found himself alone in the ruined and unpopulated city. The whole, frightful landscape was his kingdom, the rats his subjects, the graveyard his garden. But producers all over the world have a way of taking such imaginative beginnings and adding a lacquer of "commercial viability" that ends by turning them into the commonplace.

But Antoni Bohdziewicz's *Others Will Follow* developed the same theme further. So did Rybkowski's *Hours of Hope*, a story about certain prisoners who band together to get home after having been released from various German camps. Then in 1954, Ford brought out his *Five from Barska Street*, and it looked as though at last there was to be a change. For here was a film about Poland's postwar delinquents, not only an honest and realistic piece of work, but a serious study of a problem in sociology.

In the early 1950's two brilliant new directors arrived on the scene, and one of them produced the most moving war film of them all. This was *Kanal*, and the director was Andrzej Wajda, who also made *Generation*, and a film that was shown all over the world, *Ashes and Diamonds*. The second man was Jerzy Kawalerowicz who directed *The Shadow*, *A Night of Remembrance*, *Night Train*, and *The Real End of the Great War*. To these should be added the name of Andrzej Munk, killed in an automobile accident in 1961 before he had given more than a very strong promise of being perhaps the most interesting of them all.

Thus far, the great decade during which a handful of people produced a handful of what are unquestionably fine Polish films. But once they had expressed their very real horror at what had been done to them, the spring of creativity (if it did not entirely dry up) subsided considerably.

There were still individual talents, of course, men like Roman Polanski, who after *Knife in the Water* went abroad to find wider horizons for himself. Or there was Zbigniew Cybulski, candid, bitter, tragic, a Polish James Dean, if you will, who died so unnecessarily by stumbling under the wheels of a train in Wroclaw.

But they are gone, and so is the war. So is the past and the terrible readjustment. Gone too are the days of the "epic" film. They made one about the Teutonic Knights and one about Chopin, both of which Ford directed, one about Samson for Andrzej Wajda. As late as 1967 they even brought out another film about the war, a first-rate semidocumentary about the heroic Polish defense of the little spit of land called Westerplatte outside Gdansk.

But now it is all over and done with, and if you ask in Lodz what they are planning next they smile ruefully and shrug their shoulders. They are making fifteen feature films a year, but none promises to be better than run of the mill. They are grinding out an interminable television series about a Polish tank crew, and another about a mythical Captain Klos, a Polish agent in Nazi uniform. They are making seventeen "color classics in costume," all of which sounds sickeningly familiar.

The veterans have either gone abroad to make more money, or else they have simply run out of ideas. For the only fresh ideas in Poland today belong to the young, the men who have not yet settled for the peaceful life and a cottage in the country. Nor are their brains addled with ideology. They look around them, they see, they hear—and they say in public what the ordinary citizen only says to his friends.

Jerzy Skolimowski, for example, was born in 1938, so he is really too young to remember very much about the war. Wajda suggested to him that he go to the film school in Lodz. With Wajda he wrote the screenplay for *The Innocent Sorcerers* which appeared in 1960. Then he started on a career of his own with films like *Walk-over* (1965), *Barriers* (1966), and *The Start* (1967). Meanwhile he had married the pretty little actress, Joanna Szczerbic, but then, at the age of twenty-nine he made an almost unforgiveable mistake. He made a film called *Hands Up*.

Shooting it took him a mere twenty-two days. Story there was almost none. The dialogue was largely improvised, the scene a railway train. The result, Skolimowski said, was the same as if he had banged a stick into an ant heap. For the film deals with five ordinary men who, in deceptively simple little scenes, talk about modern Poland.

*Hands Up* did a rare, an entirely unexpected thing, however. It told the truth. Those who saw it were stunned and enthusiastic, for *Hands Up* was undoubtedly the work of a major talent. It was chosen for showing at the Venice Festival. But then the blow fell.

The censor forbade it to be exhibited unless certain major changes were first made to it.

Strangely enough, speech is more or less free in Poland. One may—let us say—publish a poem critical of certain aspects of Polish life. A man like Adam Schaff may even bring out a book, *Marxism and the Individual*, by no means orthodox in its opinions. These things, after all, will be read only by the few.

But so soon as the artist attempts to use one of the mass media to voice heterodox opinions he is stopped in his tracks. It would be impossible to publish a cartoon, for example, that poked fun at a Polish political leader. A novel, a play critical of Poland's relationship with the Soviet Union, would be unthinkable.

We shall have more to say about this in a moment. But the point here is that even a child can understand a film. Skolimowski's only recorded comment to the censor's demand was short and to the point. "I've seen the picture three times," he said, "and I like it as it is."

If Skolimowski goes, the Polish cinema will—at least until the real thaw comes—have ended its brief and very exciting career as it began, in silence.

# 13. Poets—Publishers—
# The Theater

O F COURSE a nation is more than the sum of its parts, and particularly is this true if the nation prides itself on being the total of many planned and well-organized efforts. For whatever virtues there may lie in organization, they almost invariably lack the power to delight or astonish us, to carry us out beyond the normal limits of awareness. Only the artist can do this, and the artist is not susceptible to being organized. Genius cannot, even if it would, fulfill the norm of a state planning commission.

We have talked, even though briefly, about the series of great Polish films—and their directors, men like Ford, Kawalerowicz, Wajda, Polanski. Lovers of the theater will have seen the work of Mrozek, or perhaps even of Rozewicz. The musician will know of the *Dies Irae* of Penderecki. But few will be aware just how bright a renaissance of all the other arts there is. From poetry to architecture, pantomime to the theater of pure experiment, the Poles are working with an intensity, an originality, and a pure joy that I, as a solitary observer, have not seen anywhere else in Europe.

And for this I think there are three main reasons. First, the enormous postwar sense of liberation into national identity; second, strong governmental support for the arts without a concomitant demand that the arts exemplify so-called Socialist realism, and third, a widespread, largely emotional desire for an individual expression long held back. As there was in the early 1950's a startling jump in the birth rate, so was there also in the number of plays and poems and pictures that were made. It was as though all Poland were shouting, "Look at us! We exist." And the artists among them were telling the rest of them why.

Nowhere is that search for identity more evident than among the poets, for they are all experimenters and belong to many schools. Most of us decry the Eng. Lit. fashion of dividing poets like so many cheeses into those that smell of Roquefort and those that more nearly resemble Camembert. Except that, like some cheeses, poems of the second class are more easily found because they are made in factories, and these are most easily described by classification.

Until 1956—silence, and then with the rout of the Stalinists, a positive explosion. Before that they had had what they called an administrative literature, which has only to pour words into the appropriate bureaucratic molds to succeed (and thereupon cease to exist). But with the liberalization (temporary though it may have been) that came in with Mr. Gomulka, influences that had lain dormant—Beckett (and Joyce, himself), John Donne, Eliot and the post-Eliot, Anglo-American positivists, the explorers into the etymological ragbag of language—burst into flower as though it were the first hot day of spring.

There was what one might call the poetry of grammar, for example, the playing with parts of words in search of fresh overtones. A man called Bialoszewski struck the imaginative spark, and within weeks he had a host of followers to whom such mathematical, crossword diagrammarianism suddenly looked the most exciting literary experiment of the decade.

A man called Jerzy Sito translated Donne, and Donne's metaphysic, as new to them and just as exciting as drink to an abstainer, started a whole new school of its own. Alongside these there came still another group, not so much neoclassicists (for that savors of the baroque) as people possessing what they thought of as a new concept of classicism itself (cousins, perhaps, of Matthew Arnold). A fourth group found itself studying, and thus harking back in its own work to the medieval Polish poetry of men like Zimorowicz, Kochanowski, and Szymonowicz. These, of course, had been good Latinists, and were themselves derivative in style. Their modern disciples were simply doing what Poles are doing in so many other fields, not only working retrospectively toward their roots, but holding those same roots up for the rest of us to look at.

They are all—all these men and women reaching toward what they hope will be a peculiarly Polish vantage point, a position from which they will be able to see with Polish eyes, different from but closely allied to the Western European tradition. For there is no such thing as Socialist poetry. Whatever else he may have been, Marx was not one of the Muses.

But men like Julian Przybos, Tadeusz Rozewicz, Mieczyslaw Jastrun are very clearly in the broad, main stream of European art. To offer translations of any of their work would be to do them an injustice. Polish poetry is romantic, sentimental, antiheroic, often bizarre, and, as Kazimierz Brandys says, the result of a love affair with the "dark and complex twentieth century." At its best it is untranslatable as the nation itself is untranslatable, being wry, pithy, introverted, strangely pragmatic, and, like the paintings of Bronislaw Linke, quite capable if you go too close of giving you a stony fist full in the face.

The prose *can* be translated, and in America the superb and gentle Polish novelist, Maria Kuncewicz, has edited an anthology, a collection of some forty pieces[1] by writers living in Poland today.

Living, I say, although one of them, Tadeusz Borowski, survived Auschwitz and Dachau only to kill himself

[1] *The Modern Polish Mind*, ed. by Maria Kuncewicz, Little, Brown, Boston, 1962.

in 1951, and another, Leszek Kolakowski, has resigned from the Party and after the student demonstrations in the spring of 1968 was discharged from his post at the university. A third, Stefan Kisielewski, had the temerity at a meeting of the Writers' Union to refer to the government as "a dictatorship of ignoramuses," upon which *Zycie Warszawy* loosed a frantic tirade of abuse against him. A fourth, Kazimierz Brandys, was one of the thirty-four writers who formally demanded an end to the censorship, and now finds it difficult to get work. Nevertheless, they are all in their particular ways alive and part of the contemporary Polish scene.

Some, like Jerzy Andrzejewski, on whose work Wajda's great film, *Ashes and Diamonds*, was based, are already well known in the West. Others, like the ineffably tender Magda Leja, are almost too young even to have much of a reputation at home. A third group, men like Klimaszewski and Tronski, darken the page in front of one's very eyes with their individual memories—like burns in the flesh—of Poland's too often generalized suffering during the war. Tronski was part of that heroic group that fought its way out of the Stare Miasto to join the insurgents in Czerniakow, and in his *Death Passed Here*, published in 1957, he brings those days vividly back to mind.

In the main, these prose writers are not experimenters, and if one may generalize (which is of course always dangerous) they are far more akin in their work to us in the west than they are to the sometimes chilling east

[ 229 ]

wind that blows over them. And this, quite apart from politics. Borowski was a Communist. Kolakowski was one of the leading Party theorists before he became disgusted with the way the Party was going. Adam Schaff, writer, philosopher, student of American Indian dialects, is actually a member of the Central Committee. But they write, they reason as we do, with none of the Party phraseology that is the death of style. If their conclusions are sometimes different from ours, they are reached by logical paths and not by way of the pot-pourri of self-deception and meaningless locution that sometimes passes even among intellectuals in the Party bureaucracy for thought.

Among the best of them, Brandys, Mrozek (who has written some delightfully funny stories), old Antoni Slonimski or his near contemporary, Jaroslaw Iwaszkie-wicz, there is often to be found that dry wit mingled with subtlety which is distinctively Polish.

Some of these, particularly the older men, hark back to the past. Others still carry the war years bitter on their tongues. But the youngest of them, Mrozek and Magda Leja, for example, are as new as and probably a good deal more vivid than the rebels of San Francisco and Notting Hill.

Polish writers who have read these remarks of mine asked why I had picked out Magda Leja for particular mention. After all, she was still under thirty; she had done comparatively little work, and in the past two or three years, practically none at all. The answer was not only that I liked the work I had seen, but that her titles, her very history were calculated to make any westerner think of her as a very close contemporary.

In 1957 she published a volume of short stories, called *The Art of Screaming*, in 1959, a novel called *The Neurotic*, and in 1960 she went on a long and what she calls "strictly private" voyage to India which turned out to be one of the most important things that had ever happened to her. In 1960 she had reached the ripe age of twenty-one.

If the writers are working with force and originality, the public are responding with an eagerness that must be heartening in the extreme. Bookshops are almost as common as tobacconists, and their stocks of contemporary work on almost every conceivable subject are enormous. On Jerozolimskie in Warsaw they even sell new books from barrows like cucumbers. There are books on art and modern Polish philosophy. There are books in French, English, German, Russian—books translated from every European language with the possible exception of the Albanian. But then, what Albanian ever wrote a book?

Poland possesses some thirty-five thousand public libraries, well over one to every thousand inhabitants. So any writer who manages to get a book into print is practically certain of a reasonable audience. So much is this true that any one of Poland's some three dozen publishers will put out a new novel in an edition of ten thousand and pay his author a royalty on the entire printing, whether it be sold out or not.

And since the average novel costs about 15 zlotys (or 35¢), the author will receive approximately 15,000 zlotys ($300) before publication, or perhaps five months' reasonable living expenses. A second printing of ten thousand will earn 80 per cent of this amount, and any subsequent printing, 60 per cent. So a Polish novel-ist, while unlikely to make a living from novels alone, will probably earn about as much in purchasing power as will his Western equivalent.

All in all, something like 6500 titles are published every year, a hundred and ten million copies, or almost four to every man, woman, and child in the country. This is indeed a change from the times before the war when a third of the population was illiterate. And inci-dentally, when one thinks of Polish fiction, one must not make the mistake of imagining it is anything like the Russian variety, full of heroic tractor drivers or stalwart Marxists doing battle against the forces of bourgeois reaction. The Poles are realists, would mostly love to be bourgeois themselves, and even if they would not, have far too lively a sense of humor.

When I was in Wroclaw in the late summer of 1967, there was an olive-cheeked enthusiast named Tadeusz Lutogniewski editing a literary monthly called *Odra*. Like its editor—a very lively man—the magazine talked theater, archaeology, politics, poetry, criticism, and its own infectious delight at Wroclaw's intellectual effervescence.

But it is a reflection of the change that has come over Poland in the past year that when I went back to Wroclaw in the spring of 1968 and asked to see Lutogniewski, I was told that he had been thrown out of his job for refusing to toe the Party line on the Arab-Israeli war. A thoroughly unpleasant gentleman called Krzyzagorski had taken his place.

I shall have more to say about Wroclaw in a moment, but up in Warsaw there is another periodical called *Dialog*, edited by Adam Tarn, and Tarn is an enthusiast of quite another sort, a man of late middle age, but still sparkling with the positive joy of discovery. As one might guess from the title, the theater is his subject, and he publishes about thirty hitherto unproduced plays a year. Many of them are inadequate. Some are even unplayable. But *Dialog* is intended to be not so much an *imprimatur* as a showcase for potentially interesting playwrights.

And of course, although he is proud of having discovered Mrozek, Mr. Tarn does not restrict himself to Polish authors. Dürrenmatt's *The Visit* came out in *Dialog* when no producer in Europe was willing to touch it. The same was true of *Waiting for Godot* and, according to Tarn, Beckett was so grateful for this encouragement when no one else showed any interest at all that he now sends *Dialog* his typescripts before they are ever shown to a producer.

[ 233 ]

The so-called Theater of Cruelty, the followers of Artaud, the Grotowski Theater in Wroclaw (of which we shall hear anon) are all anathema to Tarn. "A play is like a piece of music," he says. "Without a score it is meaningless. Ludwik Flaszen (Grotowski's literary adviser) is an invalid." This becomes more readily understandable when one realizes that Flaszen is the literary expert for a theater which as a matter of principle has nothing but contempt for the written word.

Mr. Tarn is thus a man of strong and definite opinions and very much *au fait* with theatrical happenings all over the world. One moment he will be discussing the work of a new Norwegian author, the next, illustrating his remarks with something in a Japanese No play or the experiments of a fringe group in San Francisco.

*Dialog* is his platform. There he prints, discusses, and reviews work in what is today probably the liveliest of Polish arts. There are some eighteen theaters in Warsaw alone, and very often they produce plays by contemporary European authors before they are seen in London or New York. As a matter of fact, there are theaters in Polish provincial towns doing plays that have never been seen *outside* London or New York.

As has every other nation, as has every other art, Poland has its own establishment—and its rebels against that establishment. In Warsaw, the establishment is Dejmek's National Theater. For Kazimierz Dejmek is theatrically a conservative (and a Marxist), and the repertory of the National Theater reflects his preoccupation with what he would call the peaks in theatrical tradition. Whether it still reflects his earlier Marxism is rather more open to question.

"Men like Aeschylus and Shakespeare," he says, "created their own worlds, and because they are individuals they interest me. Men like . . ." He hesitates, frowns, lights one of the innumerable cigarettes which he will stub out half smoked. "Men like Pinter, Miller, Ionesco, Osborne . . . who are they? Mirrors. Only mirrors. They reflect *our* world, and I don't need them to tell me how to look at it."

This busy, thoughtful, and intelligent man looks at one through his horn-rimmed spectacles and talks quietly, pensively, and with much deliberation about the tenets of his beliefs. Phrases stick in the mind.

"The theater of naturalism is unworthy of the best in us." (But Dejmek is a disciple of Stanislavsky.)

"Genet? Yes, his is an individual world, but one shallowly observed. Shakespeare has only two themes when you come down to it, power and love."

Or, if one asks about contemporary Poland, "The only hope in the modern Polish theater is Tadeusz Rozewicz." (But Rozewicz is far more a poet than a playwright.)

And Dejmek's productions of Slowacki, Mickiewicz, or of medieval mystery plays, indeed, of Shakespeare, are what one would hope for and expect, meticulous, imaginative, intelligent, and alive. Perhaps one reads too much between the lines, however, in recalling his production of *Dziady* (*Forefathers Eve*) in the winter of 1968. The play is by Adam Mickiewicz, and Mickiewicz is an almost sacrosanct figure in Poland, a national hero a century ago when Poland was not even a nation.

Now, a great deal happened outside the theater because of this production, and the facts ought to be put into some sort of perspective, for they are important if one is to understand the situation in Poland today. To begin with, if it were performed in its entirety, *Dziady* would be about six hours long, so in fact it has always had to be played drastically cut. In fact, there have been about fifteen productions of various sorts in the past few years, and no one has ever thought them worthy of particular comment.

But even now, months afterward, Warsaw is still full of rumors about what actually happened this time. The fact is that, for whatever reason, Dejmek included the dedicatory verses in this production, with their praise of the early nineteenth-century Russian Kolakovsky. But the Polish philosopher, Leszek Kolakowski is one of the strongest critics of the present Party hierarchy, and the mention of his name evoked spontaneous applause from the audience.

Now, Mickiewicz was not only an ardent Polish patriot, and a poet whose lyrics (as fine as anything in Wordsworth or Shelley), whose *Pan Tadeusz* and *Dziady* ought to be far better known than they are in the West. He also hated Russian tyranny with an almost self-consuming fervor. And at the very end of the play he says so. Dejmek brought a character down to the very footlights to speak the lines (thus being perfectly true to the spirit of Mickiewicz), and the speech was greeted in Warsaw with a standing ovation.

Perhaps Dejmek was as astonished as anyone else. But the authorities, unwilling (or unable) to tolerate what they considered an anti-Russian demonstration, ordered the play to be taken off. So confused is the story of what happened that no one is willing even to hazard a guess as to who signed the order. The relevant letter is said to have been lost. The production was stopped in any case (after having been very favorably reviewed, incidentally, in *Pravda*), and wittingly or not, Dejmek had struck a spark which even now has not stopped smoldering.

The Contemporary Theater in Warsaw is a different kettle of fish. Erwin Axer, who directs it, is a lively, witty individual in his late forties or early fifties. Born in Vienna, he early moved to Lwow. His father was shot in the war. Arrested, he himself escaped and actually worked as a locksmith under the Nazis, once in a house inhabited by the German Governor General, Hans Frank. In the uprising of 1944 he fought in Zoliborz until the very end, was taken prisoner by the Germans, and in the last days of the war escaped shooting only by reason of what he considers a minor miracle.

The Contemporary is a small theater; it only seats four hundred. But it has a permanent company of thirty-three and does about six plays a year—contemporary plays. One sits in Axer's office, looks round at the playbills on the walls, and there are all the names of present-day playwrights whom one respects—Ionesco, Pinter, Tennessee Williams, Beckett, Dürrenmatt, Mrozek. Axer never does one of the classics unless he feels in some particular case that he has a new approach and can say something or other that is vivid and pertinent to a modern audience.

"Who are the new playwrights in Poland?" I asked him.

"Mrozek," was the answer. "Mrozek . . . *punktum*."

To be sure, there *were* a few others. A man called Grachowiak had talent. One of the most maddening and interesting was a writer called Iredynski, who showed enormous flashes of brilliance. But he is a drunkard, a rapist, and temporarily in prison. One had hopes that—if he achieved even some momentary balance—great work might still come out of him.

Warsaw has all gradations of theater, from the Kameralny, that produced the worst *Hedda Gabler* I have ever seen, to a Jewish Theater, a "Light Opera," and a cabaret on a tiny stage in Mokotowska run by students at the university.

There a girl belts out songs with wonderful gusto. A comedy trio performs skits which are either pro-sex or anti-politics. There is the aged Party hack, for example, who delivers an incredibly boring speech to open a new town. Beside him the local chairman applauds every other banal remark with an ecstatic *"Prawda! Prawda!"*

There is the announcer on Warsaw television who reads the news with all the false enthusiasm of an automobile salesman. "The Third Secretary of the Ruthenian People's Republic," he cries joyously, "was met at the airport by the Fourth Secretary of the Moldavian People's Republic, and they issued a joint communique calling on all workers to join in the fight for peace and freedom."

Or a delegation from Rumania arrives, is listed, name after meaningless name and greeted in turn by an endless number of Polish Party officials, all of whom are listed too, and meanwhile the Fourteenth Secretary of the Wallachian People's Republic confers with the Seventh Secretary of the People's Republic of Outer Mongolia and calls on the workers of the world to unite in the struggle for peace and freedom.

The audience, mostly young, mostly students, rocked with laughter. A Party official, who had taken me to see the show, sank more and more dourly into his seat. Of course, they couldn't be taken seriously, he said. They were only students. But even he laughed at the last skit of the evening, a quiet little talk by a boy to a girl about the maxims handed down by his "uncle Charles."

"Uncle Charles says we must, simply *must* stick together, for we have nothing to lose but our chains. Darling, have you . . . have you still kept your chain, or have you . . . (shyly) have you lost it?"

I had reached this point in my narrative, when—really quite by accident—my eye fell on a copy of *Trybuna*

*Ludu* for March 6, 1968. What I read there illustrates better than anything I could say the depths of bathos to which Polish journalism has sunk. This is a quite typical news story. It is translated here verbatim.

The headline reads: POLISH-MONGOLIAN SCIENTIFIC AND TECHNICAL COMMISSION MEETS IN WARSAW.

"During March 2–4 of this year the Sixth Session of the Polish-Mongolian Commission for Scientific and Technical Cooperation met in Warsaw. During the session the fulfillment of the mutual obligations accepted at the former session of the commission was examined, as were many problems concerning the further fulfillment of scientific and technical cooperation between the two countries. The protocol signed foresees an exchange of technical documentation and leading experience in the area of the foodstuffs industry, and also the reception of Mongolian specialists for training in the Polish People's Republic.

"The session was held in an atmosphere of friendship and mutual understanding, and favored a further broadening of scientific cooperation between the Polish People's Republic and the Mongolian People's Republic.

"The protocol of the Sixth Session of the Polish-Mongolian Commission was signed by: Chairman of the Mongolian side of the commission, the first Deputy Chairman of the Commission for CEMA of the Council of Ministers of the Mongolian People's Republic, C. Davadorzh, and the Chairman of the Polish side of the commission, Deputy Chairman of the Committee for Economic Cooperation with Foreign Countries of the Council of Ministers, Antoni Czechowicz."

*Trybuna Ludu* is one of the major Warsaw newspapers.

But we were talking about theater. Of course there are theaters in every city in Poland, but it is in Wroclaw that one will find them at their most exciting and alive.

There is nothing for it but to come out with the plain truth. I love Wroclaw. I love the streets, the great, dim churches, the bridges and trees and canals, the artists, the poets, the people of this self-created city. Almost 80 per cent of it was wiped out at the end of the war, and since when it came to rebuilding, Warsaw was given priority, Wroclaw still has many broken walls and many a bare patch of earth covering some abandoned cellarage.

In 1945 there were 160,000 Germans left in Wroclaw (which of course the Germans called Breslau) and 30,000 Poles. As soon as possible the Germans were deported, and today the 30,000 have become half a million, some 40 per cent of them newly urbanized— from peasant villages all over the country.

Thus Wroclaw, like a miniature America, is composed of divergent alien elements united by a pride in their own achievements and a newly discovered local patriotism. Not only that. Wroclaw has an enormous student population possessed of all the eagerness, moved by all the ferment that being young implies. Fifty-two per cent of the inhabitants were born there since the war, so the whole city is unbelievably youthful. As a result of all these factors, individual productivity is rising more steeply there than in the rest of Poland. Their birthrate (as we saw above) is several times higher than anywhere else in the country, and the whole city is alive with ideas about town planning, the education of scientists, experimental work in a number of fields and—more than that, in an almost continual state of euphoric enthusiasm about the arts.

Most noticeably is this true of the theater, which ranges from the Polski, run by a husband and wife team, Skuszanka and Krasowski (and producing drama at as high a level as Dejmek and Axer do in Warsaw), to grand opera, the Kalambur student's theater, the world-famous Tomaszewski Pantomime, and a bizarre, avant-garde group called the Theater of Thirteen Rows (or Laboratory Theater). All of these are run by the young. All do highly professional work, and all of them receive very substantial help from the city authorities.

Henryk Tomaszewski settled in Wroclaw, he says, because it "provided an extraordinarily fertile soil for all manner of creative effort, for the new, the spontaneous, and above all the young." And his is indeed a very young theater, a theater of silence, not stylized, not literal. Indeed, Tomaszewski feels that there should always be a margin of free interpretation left to his audiences.

All modern dancing, whether it be jive and the frug or the highly complex work of Merce Cunningham or the

London School of Contemporary Dance has one thing in common and one characteristic that separates it irrevocably from dancing in the past. It is an unstylized expression either of emotion or of cerebral activity independent of story and sometimes even of music. It is more than an expression of individual talent. Fonteyn's *Giselle* may differ from Ulanova's, but they are recognizably the same ballet. The geometry of a Cunningham, on the other hand, is duplicated nowhere else on earth.

To Tomaszewski, silence is more truthful than any word, for each of us interprets a silence, a movement, a gesture in his own individual way. That, he feels, is why the pantomime is so popular among student groups. Students are too shy, indeed too inexperienced, to express themselves directly. But his theater is for them full of the symbolism, the metaphor, the rough poetry of their unspoken emotions.

His company has toured most of Europe by now with performances that are intense, colorful, macabre, and quite unlike anything else in the contemporary theater. It is entertainment, of course, but not in the old sense. It is entirely of our time, which after a long hiatus, has relearned the Aristotelian principle of the purgation of emotions through pity and fear. What we had almost forgotten was that it is we, not the actor, who must feel and perhaps even express these emotions. Tomaszewski shows us and involves us in his nostalgia, his sense of the beauty and evanescence of our own actions and emotions. With a flick of the wrist, a turn of the head, he can puzzle and frighten us as though with a sense of time passing. Leaving one of his performances, one feels wiser without knowing why; one has almost been the performer; one's own unspoken emotion has been expressed.

Jerzy Grotowski would probably not agree, or if he did, would find it unimportant that he had done so. For whereas an Axer up in Warsaw works to express his author's intention, and a Tomaszewski to affect his audience, Grotowski cares neither for the text nor for those who come to watch it being acted. He cares only for the actor himself.

His Laboratory Theater is probably one of the smallest in the world, for it can only seat thirty people and has no stage. His actors work among the audience, and they are not only acting a play. They are undergoing what amounts almost to a Freudian self-analysis in the process.

Wyspianski, Calderon, Shakespeare, all are simply means to an end. Grotowski rewrites them. Hamlet is a Jew, for that is something a modern actor can understand. The Acropolis is Poland, for Poland's blood is more real than that of the Greeks. A play takes place within a coffin where actors and audience are buried in a jumble all together. If the performance is true, if the actors fulfill Grotowski's intentions, they will at the end be able hardly to speak or stand. They will have revealed themselves, not only to the audience, but to themselves as well. They will have used themselves to the brim.

To some, Grotowski's work seems a species of theatri-

cal onanism, Flaszen's part in it an empty self-indul-
gence. To others the Laboratory Theater is an experiment from which a great deal can be learned. Erwin
Axer, who is the height of good sense, pays Grotowski a
certain grudging respect. Adam Tarn pays him none. In
the end one is inclined to the notion that interesting and
indeed moving as these performances may often be, they
do not exactly represent the final heights toward which
creation has labored.

And the Kalambur? The Kalambur plays twice
weekly to an audience of a hundred and sixty. It is, as I
said above, a student theater. The actors and technicians
have with their own hands actually made every single bit
of equipment that they use, spots, floods, dimmers—
everything. They are learning in the soundest way imag-
inable, and the only difficulty is that they so love what
they are doing that many of them have refused offers to
join professional groups.

And there, perhaps, is the secret of Wroclaw, that the
thousands of people who are working there—as actors,
poets, painters, or what you will—are doing whatever
they do not so much for money or notice or reputation,
as chiefly for sheer love of the doing. That is their secret.
It is because they are young. And that is why I, for one,
shall go back to watch them over and over again.

Almost thirty years ago when the war started, the
philosopher and painter, Witkiewicz, saddened beyond
measure at the sight of his world dying, walked out onto

an autumn hillside, sat down quietly upon the sunstruck grass, and killed himself.

That pain, that romanticism, if you will, is the old Poland. The vigorous young of Wroclaw are the new. One is tempted to believe that if any society, any ideology, any species of opportunism causes their love to be perverted or misused it will be a very great sin.

Tadeusz Rozewicz has somewhere said that his generation has knocked and been knocked about. But this new generation is still innocent and has opened its arms wide to receive the world. It deserves whatever the best is that the world can offer.

# 14. Poland 1968

Poland, unlike Rumania or Czechoslovakia, was hurt so badly that today she finds it more difficult than her neighbors to assert any ideological independence. Thus her censorship of the press, her inability to allow dissent, her unwillingness to take an independent line depend not on any teaching of Marx, but on Lenin, who had a far different cast of mind, on a Russian history of autocracy that has ingrained into its people certain habits of acceptance, a certain ineffectuality when it comes to asserting the rights of the individual when they diverge from the interests of the state. Not only Russian history has done this, not even Communist history, but Bolshevik history during its sixty years of being (in spite of its name) an embattled minority that perpetually had to close ranks against the attacks not only of reaction and imperialism, but also of those who cried out for democracy and a certain freedom of choice.

Of course, the Poles are not alone. British and American governments too have lived by lies and cynicism and double dealing. But it is damaging to one's hopes for the future if the same lies, the same disregard for human dignity are employed by a government whose whole principle was that it improved on the past, whose very *raison d'etre* was, on scientific principles, to evolve a rational society for the betterment of all our lives.

The trouble is, they have no joy in them, these people, any more than Cromwell had, or Luther, or even poor, pompous Dr. Thomas Arnold, and they, too, were all good and honorable men. The trouble is, too, that what of Marx was altered and reinterpreted by Lenin and then Stalin in the name of tactical necessity, has, like barnacles on the ship of state, considerably altered the vessel's original outlines. And the great dialectical battles long ago, with Kautsky, with Plekhanov, with Struve, even with Trotsky and (later) Dimitrov have become more important than the realities they sought to explain. It has been like a perpetual reexegesis of some Old Testament prophet while all the time the world was going on and making some of his tenets untenable. The Polish Communist Party is old, with habits of thought deeply ingrained. More than anything else in the world it is afraid of new thinking and plain fresh air. And the saddest commentary one can make is that if the truth were known, it is less afraid of the resurgence of German imperialism that it talks so incessantly about than it is of the voice of Mr. Dubcek in Prague.

It so happened that on the eighth of March 1968, I was standing in Krakowskie Przedmiescie in Warsaw just in time to see about eight or nine hundred students marching raggedly up toward Nowy Swiat from the University. They were chanting "We want freedom! We want freedom!" Bystanders watched with a certain expectant curiosity. A few policemen were walking backward, arguing with the leaders of the march. I saw no violence. It was something that has lately taken place in New York, London, Paris, Madrid, Rome, Berlin— indeed in almost every capital of the Western world.

But strangely enough, in Poland the government re- acted with unexpected anger. On the next day the dem- onstrations were even larger. Stones were thrown, a few cars were set on fire. The police went in, swinging batons, and government officials with whom I had heated discussions responded with an almost Victorian righteousness. Indeed, the world has not advanced very far since Galileo was imprisoned for maintaining that the earth went round the sun. In the Socialist states, the notion of what is "correct" so far as ideas or personal behavior are concerned, is a very close parallel to the notions of what was "correct" in the world of the widowed Victoria.

But let us go back a little and put the events of those March days into perspective. Some five weeks before, as we have seen, *Dziady* had been taken off at the National Theater. A month later, on the twenty-ninth of Febru- ary, a meeting of the Polish Writers' Union was held to protest at such governmental interference, which they called "a danger to the national culture." At that meeting men like Slonimski, Andrzejewski, Kisielewski stood up and said what a good many people had been thinking for years. Indeed, Kisielewski, a Catholic and a former member of the Sejm, made an impassioned speech that went far beyond the matter at hand.

"If they have been slapping you in the face for twenty-two years," he said, "and in the twenty-third you suddenly take offense, is that so strange? What kind of history are our children learning in school? They are learning nonsense. Matters are in the hands of ignoramuses armed with absolute, monopolistic power."

A vote was taken and a resolution condemning the government's action was carried by 221 to 124. On my later asking one of the writers present how a hundred and twenty-four people had been induced to vote on the government side, he only smiled. "You must first ask who they were," he said. "Anybody who has ever written a government handout is a member of the union."

Back in January, on the night *Dziady* was closed, a small demonstration of protest was held in the streets. Among the demonstrators were two students, Adam Michnik, a student of history, and Henryk Szlaifer, a student of political economy, who happened also to be the son of the senior censor at the Press Control office.

On the thirty-first, Michnik and Szlaifer talked to a Western correspondent, and according to a speech made late in March by Gomulka, "gave him false information which was later used in a slanderous propaganda campaign against Poland." A few days later they were dismissed from the University, and this act of dismissal became the spark that set in train all the events that followed.

And the meetings, the demonstrations were censured theoretically not because students voiced their opinions, but because they "did so illegally." They met on University property without the rector's consent, and they failed to disperse in the streets when ordered to do so by the police.

According to *Trybuna Ludu* of March 11, "Prorector Zygmunt Rybicki attempted to address those assembled in the courtyard (of the University). He recalled that the University authorities had not permitted the meeting to be called, and appealed to the young people to disperse. Some students interrupted the prorector's speech with shouts and whistles. The atmosphere of excitement and confusion became more intense. Words of abuse were heaped upon workers who arrived in the courtyard. (These were so-called Party Activists, brought in from factories by the truckload.) 'Morons,' they shouted. 'Paid flunkeys. Bandits, gestapo.' Some of the brawlers went so far as provocatively to tear up the Constitution of the Polish People's Republic."

And indeed, one can understand them. For Article 71 of the Polish Constitution reads: "The Polish People's Republic guarantees its citizens freedom of speech, of the press, of meetings and assemblies, of processions and demonstrations."

Yet on the eighth and ninth of March students were ordered to disperse. Why? They had been forbidden to meet at the University. So they went onto the streets. *There they were holding up traffic.* Where then were they expected to exercise their right to "meetings and assemblies, processions and demonstrations"?

That was the night I went to a student party in the center of town and found myself in the midst of a large, excited gathering in which at least a dozen individuals were anxious to describe just which part of the demonstrations they had seen. The air was thick with rumors. A girl had died in hospital. A pregnant undergraduate had been kicked by a policeman and arrested. She had aborted in a cell. The students of Cracow were going to rise. Such and such a factory was coming out tomorrow in sympathy.

As a matter of fact, none of these rumors was true. What *was* true, what is true to this day is that the new student generation, the generation that has known no Poland except People's Poland founded at Lublin in 1944, the youth that has benefited from its government's indubitable fostering of educational opportunity, the youth that has had no political teaching except that which it received under a Communist system, the ablest, the most intelligent, indeed, the cream of Poland's younger generation has been alienated by this government, probably beyond recall. For the same sudden blinding realization came over them as has come over the best of the young generation in all countries, that the happy things, like truth, justice, kindness, tolerance, love, are more than words, are real and tangible joys that can be reached for.

During the week of the eleventh of March there were more demonstrations, not only in Warsaw, but in Lublin, in Poznan, in Gdansk, and in other centers. The police as well as activist groups out of nearby factories were called in and dispersed them. By this time, too, it had become plain that the demonstrations were not entirely spontaneous. They had their leaders and their organizers, and whenever these were boys or girls of Jewish origin, this fact was pointed out in the press. Whenever leaders were sons or daughters of prominent people, these people were dismissed from their posts. So Eduard Ochab fell as Head of State because his daughter had taken part in the demonstrations. The fact that Ochab and his daughter were hardly on speaking terms did not help him in the slightest.

The government's reaction was psychologically if not politically understandable. In spite of the generalizations of the ignorant, Communists have an honest love for books, for music, for theater, for education. Upon the devastation of 1945 they built technical schools and universities. In 1966 there were over eight million students in Poland of one sort or another. In 1967–68 there were 287,000 boys and girls in colleges and universities, six times as many as before the war. The state budget for education in 1968 comes to fifteen billion zlotys ($300,-000,000), and a third of this is earmarked for tertiary schooling. As with things artistic and historical, the Poles have made very conscious efforts to demonstrate how false were the terrible and shaming things the Germans said about them. The young were to be their hope. The young were their future. From their earliest years, children were sent to holiday camps—to lake or forest—when no other group could afford it. From their earliest years, children have after-school play and hobby groups. They are taught to make everything from radios to sailboats. They have whole little natural history museums built for them in the youth centers. They do theater and mime. They form ballet and choral groups. It was for the young that all the postwar privations were undergone. And now this youth had flown in the face of what it had been taught. It had demanded the right to think for itself. It had grown sick of censorship and conformity and looking only in one direction. It had made itself part of that unorganized conspiracy of youth all over the world that has broken out in rebellion against doublethink and doubletalk, opportunism and downright lies. It was one with the youth of America that had no use for Johnson and Humphrey, the youth of Britain that has nothing but derision for Wilson, Heath, or any other head of an establishment, the youth of Germany that has risen in revulsion not only against its adult leaders, but against the whole terrifying world out of which they sprang.

And the Polish Party leaders could think of no answer except a demand for discipline. They felt shocked and betrayed. Thus far the picture is clear enough. But there was more to it than that. Even during the first days, before the official explanation was published, rumors of every sort flickered round Warsaw, and in most of them the name Moczar cropped up. General Mieczyslaw Moczar had fought in the Communist AL during the war and, as Minister of the Interior and head of the Secret Police, is generally thought of as Poland's "strong man."

When students were beaten up in prisons, people said, "Ah! It's an attempt by Moczar (who controlled the police) to make Gomulka unpopular." From the very start it seemed evident to most observers that there was a wide split in the Central Committee, with Gomulka, Gierek, and Spychalski on one side, and Moczar and certain unnamed confederates on the other.

And then, because it was unthinkable that students, writers, and intellectuals could all have abandoned the government, there had to be an official explanation. And very quickly indeed that explanation was made. Certain Stalinists, in collaboration with Zionists and German revanchist circles, had misled a few gullible students and caused them to neglect their duty and demonstrate against the authorities. Certain Party members, discredited by Gomulka in 1956, had plotted to regain power, and had used their sons and daughters as naive pawns in the name of political revisionism.

[ 255 ]

Now of course, anyone may rattle Stalin's ghost with impunity. It was also safe to blame the Germans. But both Stalinists and Germans are comparatively rare on the ground in Poland, and someone had to be found who could be publicly blamed without doing any real harm. What handier enemy than (not really the Jews, but) the Israelis?

Here is what *Slowo Powszechny* of March 10 had to say:

The alliance contracted between the state of Israel and the German Federal Republic, an alliance which has been revealed particularly in recent years, is no secret to any politically informed person. This alliance implies not only the services of Germany to Israel, but also the other way round. These services, rendered by Israel and Zionism to Germany have been revealed in a broad campaign which, on the one hand, is intended to provide a certificate of good conduct to the present German authorities and to clear them of their Hitlerite, criminal past and, on the other hand, to defame the underground struggle of the Polish nation against the Hitlerite occupant and to shift the responsibility for the murder of six million Jews in concentration camps onto the Polish nation. At the same time this campaign aims at undermining the authority of the political leadership of People's Poland, particularly the authority of Wladyslaw Gomulka, who is the embodiment of the only correct international policy defining the position and security of Poland in the world. The Zionists in Poland accepted this political demand of the Federal German Republic all the more willingly since they cannot forgive Wladyslaw Gomulka for his evaluation, correct from the point of view of world peace and Poland's interests, of the Israeli aggression against the Arab countries last June.

If Zionists making common cause with Germans to blame Poland for Hitler's murder of the Jews—if this seems an unlikely partnership and an unlikely goal, it is at least equaled by the theory of a Party spokesman who, to my objection that it was unlikely for Stalinists to go marching down the road, shouting, "We want freedom!" interjected, "But don't you see? They shout that just to mislead people. There, whether you believe it or not, is the *proof* that they are Stalinists."

Meanwhile, students who had been arrested were given savage sentences. Suddenly it became almost impossible for a student to be granted a passport. More and more were called up into the army on the pretext that since certain faculties at the University had been closed down, they were no longer students.

For two or three years, the fine false dawn Gomulka had brought with him in 1956 had been visibly fading. Now, as though the student demonstrations were a signal, the government acted on a wide variety of fronts to stifle any possible opposition. Production of a new play by Mrozek was postponed. Leszek Kolakowski, a brilliant Party theoretician and the darling of Polish youth in 1956, Wlodzimierz Brus, the world-renowned economist who advocated reforms adopted in Hungary and Czechoslovakia (but not in Poland), and four other professors at Warsaw University were dismissed. *Trybuna Ludu* stated on March twenty-sixth that "the highest interests of the state and the nation require that they should be barred from influencing the education of the young."

In April, the Director of the Lodz film studios was thrown out of his job. Then came the turn of Aleksander Ford, the *doyen* of Polish film directors (Wajda was already abroad; so, of course, was Polanski). Early in May, six separate editors of *Zycie Warszawy* were either dismissed or resigned their posts. In Lodz, ten newspapermen were expelled from the Party. Soon after, Mr. Wladyslaw Wedrowski, head of State Farms for the province of Warsaw, was discharged for tolerating "compromised persons" on his staff. He was forbidden to hold another managerial post for at least three years. By mid-May well over a hundred people formerly prominent in the professions (sometimes in the army) had been thrown out of their jobs.

One category of persons who cannot of course be dismissed is that which started the whole minor rebellion. I mean, of course, the writers. Instead, they suffered under positively virulent attacks in the press. Slonimski (who is a Jew) is labeled an anti-Semite. Jasienica is called a Fascist murderer. As for Kisielewski, *Zycie Warszawy*, on March fourteenth, attacked him with such disorganized, blind fury that the article is almost incoherent. Everything from Vietnam to Churchill and Cardinal Spellman is brought in, and fourteen times the epithet he had used—"a dictatorship of ignoramuses" is thrown in his face, so that at the end it is indeed the only phrase one remembers. Very shortly afterward, Mr. Kisielewski was attacked in the street by some thugs who were never identified. At about the same time someone or other exploded a tear gas bomb in the censor's office. He was never found either, and it is an interesting commentary on the inefficacy of censorship that although neither of these stories appeared in the press half Warsaw knew about them in a matter of hours.

I had a long talk during those days with a writer of great eminence. Out of doors the snow fell softly over a silent park. In the room friends and students softly came, listened, now and then threw in a remark.

The writer talked of the future, and pointed out sadly that there was no political figure they could trust. Poland had no Dubcek visible in the offing, and a regime that equated tactical necessity with objective truth could not allow revisionism. Marx and Engels had allowed none of that nonsense. It was Lenin who had started it with his intolerance of opposition.

"How on earth," he asked quietly, almost rhetorically, "can political necessity govern objective fact?"

In the long run, of course, liberalization had to come. "But tell them abroad," he said. "Tell them abroad that it is more difficult to conduct the orchestra than to listen to the music."

All during those days, the older generation most often watched—not without approval—and sat on its hands. "I'm buying a car," one journalist said to me. "How can I possibly afford to lose my job?" That was a fairly

widespread point of view. They ignored what they read
in the papers, for they knew it to be meaningless. They
snorted with derision at the government's boast of continued economic progress, for in spite of enormous
achievements and indeed admirable planning, they saw
around them now too many examples of incompetence
and inefficiency, and suspected that, unlike the Czechs
and Hungarians, they had reached virtual economic
stagnation.

Strangely enough, unpopular though the Russians
may be, almost no one questions the desirability of a
Russian alliance. Hardly anyone desires to change the
system. But almost everyone would like to see now the
economic reform and the democratic liberalization
which seem in the long run to be inevitable.

In the absence of any real revolt, it is all the more
strange to see the government reacting to events with
what can only be described as panic. The overtones of
anti-Semitism are an example, for Polish Communists are
most emphatically not anti-Semitic, and this in spite of
the almost ludicrous and indeed inflammatory headlines
in Western papers. Mr. Gomulka's wife is Jewish. Karl
Marx, himself, was born a Jew. And if you attack the
Party for what seem to be anti-Jewish strictures in its
press, its spokesmen will defend themselves with all the
righteous indignation of the misunderstood.

Before the outbreak of the Arab-Israeli war, Poland
had a flourishing trade with Israel. After it, she broke off
diplomatic relations. In this, of course, she was simply

hewing to the Russian line. Indeed, at the time of that war, people often remembered that many Israelis had formerly been Poles, and a remark often heard in Warsaw was, "Isn't it marvelous how our Jews are beating up their (the Russians') Jews?" In the convoluted Communist world, to fail to support the Arabs became equivalent to attacking the Soviet Union.

Now, many Polish Jews (and there are only about thirty thousand left in the country) were of course delighted by the Israeli victory. People who expressed that delight became, by definition, enemies of the Russians, thus enemies to Poland, thus suspect of being engaged in heaven knows what Machiavellian plots and subterfuges.

"When a Jew is thrown out of his job," one man said to me, "your press raises a hue and cry about our anti-Semitism. But when we dismiss a Party member, no one says that we are anti-Party or anti-Polish."

And this, I think, is fair comment, no matter how unfair, how unwise, or how illiberal may be Polish interpretations of what constitutes loyalty to the state. Indeed, on the tenth of April, the Prime Minister, Mr. Cyrankiewicz, in a speech to the Sejm about the recent demonstrations, roundly attacked those who accused the government of anti-Semitism. "It is we Poles," he said in effect, "who saved whatever Jews were saved from the crematoria. It is we Poles, not the international bankers, who fought in the ghetto. And if tens of thousands of people managed to escape from that hell, it was only because they found help and material assistance among the Polish people."

But, when Poland and Israel stood in opposing camps, he went on, Poles had to decide where they belonged. It is impossible at the same time to be loyal to Socialist Poland and imperialist Israel. Here a choice must be made. He who comes to the conclusion that he should emigrate will not find any obstacles put in his way.

"Who could question the Polishness," he asks, "of Szymon Askenazy, Marceli Handelsman, Grzegorz Fitelberg, Professor Ludwik Hirszfeld, Julian Tuwim, Adolf Warski, Feliks Perl, and many others? Polish culture, Polish science, the Polish progressive and revolutionary movement would be so much poorer without them, and there are many people like these among us, born on this soil, brought up in our culture, for whom Poland is their only and indisputable homeland."

It must be admitted that this does not sound like anti-Semitism, and if there be those who would insist that Mr. Cyrankiewicz is pulling the wool over our eyes, they do rather remind one of the accusation that the Stalinists shout "We want freedom" only to mislead us.

Today Poland's adherence to the Soviet alliance has become as much an emotional as a practical necessity. Years spent plotting in opposition have trained them to see plots and counterplots where none exist, and a certain viability in the economy won only at the cost of enormous sacrifice has made them preternaturally fearful of an economic liberalization that might endanger it.

As I said at the very beginning, writing about Poland is like walking on eggs. Nothing is entirely true or entirely untrue, but for reasons which by now should have become apparent, Polish Communists, Polish non-Communists, emigre Poles full of nostalgia, emigre Poles who loathe all Poland stands for, people who want to believe well of any Socialist state, people who feel nothing but an irrational hatred for one—all of these will dispute whatever conclusions one draws with a positively unanswerable emotionalism.

So I shall draw no conclusions. They are inherent in what I have already set down—about industry, about the land, the Church—the good and the bad, the failures and the achievements. That there is much good I think there can be no question. In some respects their achievements have been almost miraculous, particularly when one remembers not only the natural handicaps under which they labored, but also the handicaps they invented for themselves.

Let me end with one thought directed to my friends in Poland. Peter the Great established the internal passport in Russia as a symbol, almost, of the power of bureaucracy over the individual. Its purpose was to keep the serf on the land or in whatever place he was wanted. The Russian revolution abolished the internal passport as "a police instrument of oppression of the masses." In 1932 Stalin brought it back. People carry them in Poland today.

This is a little thing, Polish friends have said to me.

But it is an accumulation of little things, of little freedoms that make the big freedom.

And one other thought. In 1918 the great Polish Communist revolutionist, Rosa Luxembourg, lay in prison in Breslau, and there she wrote: "The public life of countries possessing limited freedom is so poverty-stricken, so miserable, so rigid, so unfruitful precisely because through the exclusion of democracy it cuts off the living sources of all spiritual riches and progress . . . Without general elections, without unrestricted freedom of press and assembly, without a free struggle of opinion, life dies out in every public institution. Only the bureaucracy remains as the active element.

"Freedom," she wrote, "freedom only for the supporters of the government, freedom only for the members of one party—however numerous they may be—is no freedom at all. Freedom is always and exclusively for the one who thinks differently. Not because of any fanatical concept of abstract justice, but because everything that is instructive or wholesome or purifying in political freedom depends on this essential characteristic, and because all the virtue of it vanishes when freedom becomes a thing to be granted or denied."

The virtue, the intelligence, the humanity of rulers can never be judged except in relation to their people's needs. Poland's rulers, if judged by comparison with their contemporaries elsewhere in the world, are in the main honest, humane, and of good will. But if judged by the real aspirations of the best of their countrymen they are woefully in arrears.

Not one of them stands in the living stream of public hope or desire. Not one of them, like Tito or Kennedy or Churchill or Castro or perhaps even Mr. Dubcek, tries to represent the conscience of his race.

# Postscript

As we went to press, the sad and perhaps inevitable happened, and Czechoslovakia was invaded. The world expressed its shock in the well rehearsed phrases that the world reserves for these occasions. The cynical shrugged their shoulders. They knew all the time. America was brutalizing Vietnam in the name of *status quo*. The Russians were using a little less violence to protect their own sphere of influence. So on both sides the unspoken gentleman's agreement was maintained—that is, if one can call such adversaries gentlemen. The emotional perhaps felt tears in their eyes. The romantic talked about Masaryk. General De Gaulle predictably blamed it all on the Yalta agreement, which France, of course, had not signed. Unimportant that she had not even been asked to sign. Words are used for their effects, not for their meanings. The West Germans threw up their hands in holy and righteous horror. The East Germans actually marched, as they had done under Hitler only a generation before.

By the time this is read the United Nations will have passed a compromise resolution, compromise because some measure of *détente* must be preserved for all our sakes. The Pope will have expressed his guarded unhappiness, guarded lest a more forthright statement be harmful to Catholics in Poland. It was ever thus. German revanchist circles will proclaim jubilantly that they were right all the time. Cold warriors from Berlin to San

Francisco will smile at this seeming justification of their policies. But in Poland (and this is a book about modern Poland), I know not half a dozen people who will have greeted the news with anything but sadness and despair.

For the truth is that (more than any ideology) it is we as individuals who have suffered the almost traumatic defeat, right-wing individuals as well as left, we Western as well as the Russian, social democratic as well as what Moscow likes to call Marxist-Leninist.

The truth is that we have had a barrier put to our aspirations, for now the individual is no longer important, whether here or in the East. In Germany, in America, to a lesser extent in Britain, the individual has long been little more than a market-ing unit, a gullet that needs feeding, a body that needs clothing, housing, transporting and providing with as much medicinal pap and prepacked pleasure as it can be induced to swallow—all in the interests of higher company profits. In the so-called Socialist states he is an integer of another sort, an underpaid, undertrained, undervalued and completely unindividual unit in the service of a state that as far as one can tell has no function except to exist.

The West is perhaps the slightly more preferable organism because at least it provides many of its proles with a greater degree of comfort and the illusion of importance. The East has committed the greater betrayal because it started by making the greater promises.

Now the Soviet Union has effectively reseized Czechoslovakia. People who perhaps sought entrance into a third world have been denied that opportunity. But let no one be glad or proud at having been right—least of all Germans or Americans. For it was Americans who with their dread of change and their national self-assertiveness made a division of the world into spheres of influence inevitable, and it was the Germans who with their brutality and their ridiculous righteousness invited the current antihumanists into Europe in the first place—almost thirty years ago.

*August 22, 1968.*

# Index

# INDEX

# INDEX

# Index

Poznan, 35, 74, 75, 109, 116, 121, 122, 129, 130, 156, 186, 189; art show in, 215–216; described, 144–145; International Trade Fair at, 144, 145; protest march in, 151–152; student demonstrations in, 253

"Poznan Larks" (choir), 144

Praga, 61, 62, 72, 84, 90, 97 *n.*

Prague, 146

Prejss, Mr., x

Press Control office, 250

Przetakiewicz, Zygmunt, 205–206

Przybos, Julian, 228

Publishing industry, 231–232, 233; wartime underground, 35–37

Pulawy, 132, 152, 156, 157, 190

Radom, 26, 30, 131

"Radoslaw" armed group, 87, 88, 91

RAF, 8, 9, 21, 22, 61, 62

*Real End of the Great War, The* (film), 221

Red Army, in Poland, 61–63, 72, 84, 92, 94, 96, 97, 109, 113

Reiff, Ruszard, 205

Reinefarth, Heinz, 69, 73 and *n.*, 74–75, 79 and *n.*, 80

*Rise and Fall of the Third Reich, The* (Shirer), 4

Rode, Ernest, 74 *n.*

Roosevelt, Franklin D., 62; quoted, 104–105

Rowecki, Lt. General, 52

Rozewicz, Tadeusz, 225, 228, 235, 246

Rozinska, Janina, quoted, 76

Ruczay, Major, 70

Rumania, 37, 166, 247

Rundstedt, General, quoted, 73

Russia, *see* Soviet Union

Rutkowski, Adam, 28 *n.*

Rybicki, Zygmunt, 251

Rybkowski, Mr., 221

Rybnik, 139–142

Rydz-Smigly, Marshal, 120

Rzeszotarski, Mr., 124; quoted, 125

Sachsenhausen, 32, 35, 52

St. Barbara's day, in Rybnik, 141

*Samotność (Loneliness)* (ballet), 217

Satire, political, 238–239

Sawicki, Jerzy, 74 *n.*

Schaff, Adam, 224, 230

*Schleswig Holstein* (cruiser), 4

Schmidt, Janina, 194, 211

Schneider, Gerda, 220

Schopenhauer, Arthur, 125

Sculpture, 194, 211, 213, 216

Seibert, Mr., 194

Serov, General, 204

*Seventy Days* (Zagorski), 62, 72, 91

*Shadow, The* (film), 221

Shakespeare, William, 235, 244

Shipbuilding, 154–156, 168

Shirer, William L., 4 and *n.*

Shulman, Milton, 73 *n.*

*Sign, The (Znak)*, 199

Sikorski, General, 21, 37, 203

Silesia, 104, 105, 136–138, 152

Silesian rebellion (1921), 6, 137

Sito, Jerzy, 227

Skiwski, Emil, 19

Skolimowski, Jerzy, 223, 224

Slonimski, Antoni, 230, 250, 258

Slonimski, Lucja and Stefan, 28

*Slowo Powszechny*, 205; quoted, 256

Sobanski, Tomasz, 44–48

Sobieski, Jan, 133, 148

Socialism, in Poland, 50, 140; and art, 214, 226; and Catholic Church, 196, 200–210; defects of, 170–172; virtues of, 163–164; *see also* Communism; Marxism

*Soldek* (ship), 154–155

Soviet Union, 60, 186, 196, 203, 217, 265–266 and Katyn Forest massacre, 19–20, 60; Poland's relationship with, 21, 82, 120, 139, 165, 224, 260–262

*Spiegel, Der*, 79 and *n.*

Spychalski, Mr., 139, 255

Stalin, Josef, 60, 62, 147, 151, 201, 248, 256, 263

Stalinism, and Poland, 226

Stare Miasto (Old Town), Warsaw, 7, 65, 87, 130, 229; restoration of, 148, 195

*Start, The* (film), 223

Starzynski, Mayor, of Warsaw, 4, 5

State farms, 127, 145–146, 180, 182–185

Stawinski, Jerzy Stefan, 87 *n.*

Steel production, 138, 154, 168, 172

Stocznia Gdanska, 155

Stomma, Professor, 192

Stroop, Jürgen, 30 *n.;* quoted, 30

Studnicki, Wladislaw, 19

Sulphur mining, 152, 154, 165, 168

Swiatlo, Jozef, 204

Szandorowska, Janina, 28

Szczecin (Stettin), xi, 104, 108, 121–123, 143, 156

Szczerbic, Joanna, 223

Szewczyk, Wilhelm, 138, 140

Szlacheta, Waclawa, quoted, 77

Szlaifer, Henryk, 250

Szmanski, Stanislaw, 217

Szmulewski, David, 38

*Sztafeta*, 203

Szymanowska, Maria, 215

Szymonowicz, Szymon, 227

# INDEX

Tannenberg (Grünwald), battle of, 1, 211
Tarlo-Mazinski, Mr., 18
Tarn, Adam, 233–234, 245; quoted, 234
Television, 163, 217–218, 222, 239
Textiles, 136, 138, 153, 167, 169
Theater: of cruelty, 234; in Katowice, 137; pantomime, 226, 242; in Warsaw, 147, 234–239, 242, 244, 249; wartime underground, 35; in Wroclaw, 143–144, 241, 242–245
Theater of Thirteen Rows, 242, 244–245
Thorvald, J., 102 *n.*
Tito, Marshal, 265
Tomaszewski, Henryk, 243–244; quoted, 242
Tomaszewski Pantomime theater, 242
Topolski, Feliks, 174
Treblinka, 24, 32, 38 and *n.*, 44
Tronski, Mr., 229
*Trybuna Ludu*, 239–241; quoted, 251, 257–258
Trzesniewska, Krystyna, 41–42, 43
Tuetonic Knights, 2, 126, 222
Tuwim, Julian, 262
*Twenty Years of Poland's Economic Development, 1944–64* (Karpinski), 172 *n.*

Union of Journalists, Polish, 205–206
United Nations, 265
United States of America, 119, 145, 165, 166, 174, 213, 248, 265–266
*Universal Weekly*, 199
University of Cracow, 34, 137–138, 211
University of Warsaw, 19, 249, 250–251, 257
*Unvanquished City* (film), 220

Vatican Ecumenical Council, 198, 201
*Verbrennungskommando Warschau* (Klimaszewski), 79
Vienna, 14, 146
Vietnam, 171, 213, 258, 265
Vistula River, 2, 7, 25, 121, 233

*Waiting for Godot* (Beckett), 233
Wajda, Andrzej, 87 *n.*, 221, 222, 223, 225, 229, 258
*Walkover* (film), 223
Wantula, Leon, quoted, 140
Warsaw: destruction of, 1, 16, 93–94; as Paris of the East, 2, 7; plunder of, by Germans, 14–17; restoration of Stare Miasto in, 148, 195; siege of, 64–93;

student demonstrations in, x, 249, 251–257; television in, 217–219, 239; theater in, 147, 234–239, 242; University of, 19, 249, 250–251, 257; wartime life in, 7–13, 23–24
Warsaw Castle, 7, 15 and *n.*, 16
*Warsaw Robinson Crusoe, A* (Andrzejewski), 220–221
Warski, Adolf, 262
Warta River, 121, 144, 146
*Wave, The* (*Fala*), 36
Wawel Castle, 133
Wedrowski, Wladyslaw, 258
Wieliczka salt mines, 134
Wielkopolska, 130, 145, 180
Wieniawski competition, in music, 144
Wilanow palace, 148
Wilno, 97, 104
Witkiewicz, S., 245–246
Wittenberg, Iccak, 30
Wojtyla, Cardinal, 35, 198, 199, 209
Wola, 65, 69, 75, 87, 93, 146–147
Wolak, Mr., 194
Writers, contemporary, 228–231, 258–260
Writers' Union, Polish, 229, 249–250
Wroclaw (Breslau), xi, 99, 106, 108, 109, 111, 121, 122, 195, 241–246; Artists' Club in, 144; theater in, 143–144, 241, 242–245
Wyszynski, Stefan Cardinal, 142–143, 198–199, 200–201, 207; quoted, 194–195

Yalta, 104, 265

Zagorski, Karol, 67–68
Zagorski, Waclaw, 62 *n.*, 72 and *n.*, 91, 92, 93
Zakopane, 124, 134
Zaluski, Zbigniew, 83–86, 86 *n.*, 88, 89, 91 *n.*; quoted, 86
Zamosc concentration camp, 39–41
Zarzychi, Jerzy, 220
*Zburzenie Warszawy*, 74 *n.*
Zelazowa Wola, 148–149
*Ziemianska* (Dugout), in Warsaw, 53
Zietek, Jerzy, 136–137
Zionists, x, 139, 255–257
"Znachor," in Lublin, 30
*Znachnor*, in Warsaw, 53
ZNAK, 192, 199, 201
Zoliborz, 68, 69, 85, 87, 88, 91
*Zycie Warszawy*, 229, 258–259